# Master your Fly Casting!

### ...and have fun doing it

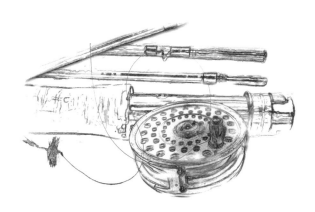

# About the author

JIM C. CHAPRALIS was the pioneer in the international fishing travel business. In 1961/62 he established the Fishing Division for Safari Outfitters, Inc. In 1975, he founded PanAngling Travel Service. Jim and his staff booked more than 40,000 international fishing trips for anglers and explored, developed and marketed numerous fishing areas around the globe. He has fished in about 40 countries.

Jim has written dozens of articles for major fishing and outdoor magazines and several books including *World Guide to Fly Fishing, Fishing Escapes* (co-author) and, most recently, *FISHING PASSION:A lifelong love affair with angling.*

Jim was elected to the original *Fishing Hall of Fame* and is a recipient of the *Dolphin Award* for his contributions to international fishing.

He won the International Distance Fly Casting Championship (Paris, France, 1955) and the All-Round Casting Championship (Stuttgart, Germany, 1956). After a hiatus of more than 40 years, Jim returned to tournament casting and has won a number of Gold, Bronze and Silver Medals (Senior's Division) in recent ACA Nationals.

Although he fished most of the great places in the world, Jim is now addicted to Central Wisconsin stream trout fishing.

His varied background includes guiding for one year in Ontario, manufacturing and importing fishing tackle (Sportackle International), editing a regional outdoor publication and serving as a fishing consultant for an encyclopedia company.

# Master your
# Fly Casting!
### ...and have fun doing it

by Jim C. Chapralis

graphics/illustrations: *Design by Dimitri*

**AnglingMatters Press**
P.O. Box 4938
Skokie, IL 60076-4938

Printed in the United States of America
10 9 8 7 6 5 4 3 2
Master Your Fly Casting! ...and have fun doing it
by Jim C. Chapralis
Library of Congress Control Number: 2005905309
ISBN: 978-0-97086536-6


**Editors:** Elaine Fiedler and Sally Chapralis
**Graphics:** DESIGN BY DIMITRI

**COVER PHOTO**
*Peter Aravosis casts a large streamer*
*in South America for*
*the freshwater dorado.*

# Table of Contents

# SECTION TWO

# SECTION THREE

# Dedication

To Sally . . . for her understanding (I'm sure
it isn't easy being married to an angler and
an addicted distance caster), encouragement,
patience and her straight talk. (*"Jim, you need to
practice your Levels more . . . and better start
with Level One!"* — after watching me cast in
our back yard.)

OTHER BOOKS BY JIM C. CHAPRALIS

*World Guide to Fly Fishing*

*Fishing Escapes* (co-author Paul Melchior)

*Fishing Passion: A lifelong love affair with angling*

# Fly fishing . . . everyone?

EVERY YEAR thousands of men and women are attracted to fly fishing. Many were inspired by Robert Redford's classic movie of Norman Maclean's *A River Runs Through It*. I know this is true because at our fishing travel office we received many calls from people who saw the film then and wanted to take up fly casting. "It looks so cool . . . the way the line unfolds back and forth," would be a typical comment. Probably about 20 to 30 percent of the calls were from women.

Not only did *A River Runs Through It* attract direct interest to fly fishing, but it also influenced the media to use fly casting as a background motif in electronic and print ads.

Fly fishing was definitely "in."

People flocked to tackle stores to learn about fly casting and to buy the necessary equipment. They attended sport shows and watched casting demonstrations. How-to fly cast books were gobbled up by hopefuls. The movie spawned many new fly-fishing schools, dedicated outdoor shows, several fly-fishing magazines and hundreds of fly shops.

Many neo-anglers, decked out in brand-new waders and the latest in fly-fishing apparel, suddenly appeared on trout streams everywhere.

At a celebrated Latin American light-tackle spa, I asked an attractive thirtyish woman whether she was fly fishing.

"Oh, is there another form of fishing?" she said, not at all attempting to disguise her obvious snobbishness.

In my book, *FISHING PASSION: a Lifetime Love Affair with Angling,* I included a chapter called "Michael's Great Bonefish Adventure." Michael was a very successful young man, who decided to take up fly fishing for bonefish. I had not met Michael before and we were paired to fish together at a Bahamian bonefish camp. I've never seen a better equipped angler, and this was his very first fishing trip! He explained that he had been attracted to fly fishing after viewing several television fishing programs. He thought he needed a hobby, an escape of sorts, from his work, and his wife encouraged him to pursue fly fishing.

I thought Michael was doing well—he was first up at the deck—but soon he ordered our guide to take him back to the lodge. Suddenly he didn't like fly fishing. He packed and went home. Just like that.

While Michael's bonefishing adventure is unique, it is also true that many people who were attracted to fly fishing and fly casting never went through the normal fishing progression that most of us old-timers experienced: First we learned to fish with a cane pole, then with a bait casting or spinning outfit, followed by using artificial lures and finally fly fishing. I believe there is a better sense of appreciation that way.

But today, many—especially younger people or the "now generation"—want to get into fly fishing immediately. Of course, they realize that in order to fly fish, they must learn to fly cast. They do so via several avenues:

1) They sign-up for a fly-fishing/fly-casting course offered at the many fly fishing schools across the country.

2) They may have a fly-fishing friend teach them the basics.

3) They may teach themselves by viewing the various videos or by reading some of the fly-casting books.

4) They may obtain a fly-casting lesson at one of the sport shows or at a tournament casting club, or

5) The majority of newcomers to fly casting that I've met have taken a casting course with one of the fly shops.

***This book is not intended to teach you the basics of fly casting.*** There are many superb books and instructors who teach you that.

Instead, the goal of this book is to take the novice fly caster—casters who have had some instruction and can perform a simple fly cast—through a series of casting programs and transform him/her into a good, excellent or superb caster. The level of acquired and retained expertise depends on the novice. Similarly, it will help the intermediate fly caster to become an expert, and, if willing to devote the necessary time, enter that rarefied class that holds the upper ten percent of fly casters.

The lessons or levels are designed to progress from novice all the way to a master level.

We operate as a team. I will provide the various casting events/games/disciplines that I believe are necessary to fulfill our goals, and you need to practice them and advance from level to level ***only*** when you master or conquer the event.

Practice is not a user-friendly word to most of us. Be assured that once you get the hang of these disciplines, most of you are going to love these games. Many of you will find these games not only fun but perhaps addictive.

Some of you will find them so challenging that they may bring out your competitive juices. You may challenge fishing pals in friendly competition: Who can cast farther or who can cast more accurately or both? You may want to start a casting club. I'll tell you how in this book.

You may want to compete in local, organized casting tournaments. I'll provide you with the rules and casting schemes. You may even want to enter World Casting Championships!

Okay, okay, we're ahead of ourselves. One step at a time.

*Will your cast land too short? Will you dump that leader like a batch of cooked spaghetti on the trout's head?*

*Or make that perfect cast and be amply rewarded.*

*It's up to you!*

# Why do we need to practice?

L ET ME START off by giving you the most basic but often ignored fact for successful fishing: Aside from still fishing, jigging or trolling, **casting skill is the most important determining factor in fishing success**. This is especially true in fly fishing.

You can obtain the best fishing gear that money can buy and reserve prime time at a storied trout river or fishing lodge, but if you are a poor caster, your results will suffer.

Suppose you're on a Montana blue-ribbon trout stream and your guide points out a big brown. You know, the kind that has spots almost as large as your thumbnail!

Even the guide is excited as he whispers his strategy: "Ya gotta put that fly about five feet above him, in his feeding lane. Don't cast over him 'cuz he'll spook. If you cast too far ahead of him, you'll have drag. He's a big fella, I'll tell ya. And don't slap the fly down hard. Go ahead!"

Geez! So there you are. Waist deep in swirling currents. The big trout is sipping flies methodically.

*Slurp.* Pause. *Slurp.* Pause. Pause. *Slurp*!

You paid $590 for that graphite rod, the one that's shaking in your trembling hand, 200 bucks for the fly reel, and hundreds of dollars for lines, flies, waders and other incidentals. And, of course, there may be lodge expenses, the airline tickets and the guide. A small fortune.

Your guide is watching you closely as you lengthen your cast.

*The moment of truth.*

You.

The fish.

The quivering rod.

The trout.

The big trout. Perhaps a "lifetime trout."

Can you make that cast? Will your cast land too short? Will you dump that leader like a batch of cooked spaghetti on the trout's head?

Maybe you'll make that perfect cast, and the fish will rise to the fly.

*Maybe.*

Perhaps you're in the Keys and your guide spots a tarpon about 80 feet away. The wind is blowing the wrong way (it *always* is, at critical times). You will need to double haul. Maybe with only one false cast make a 70- to 80-foot cast. Will you be able to make that cast?

Or let's magically place you on a pristine bonefish flat in the Bahamas. *Zoom!* You're there! Perfect conditions. You've located a big bone tailing, but no matter how much *oomph* you put into the cast you're 10—15 feet short. You move up closer. Your cast is still short. But the fish is still tailing. You creep a few yards closer . . . and the fish spooks!

Or you're on a bass lake. A largemouth just fed voraciously under that overhanging oak. Maybe it captured a frog out for a little afternoon swim. Big fish, too. You need to deliver that bass bug just under those branches, and if you do, you know you'll be rewarded with a vicious strike. Can you make that cast? Or will you hang up?

This is not going to be a how-to-cast book. Thankfully, there are lots of great books on casting. By Joan Wulff, Lefty Kreh, Mel Krieger, Jason Borger . . . to name just a few. Video tapes, too.

There are a number of excellent Web sites that dispense with good casting tips for free.

There are hundreds—perhaps thousands—of fly-casting schools across the country. Tackle manufacturers, fly shops and qualified individuals regularly conduct these schools.

Many hopefuls go to these casting seminars, and most learn to cast well enough to catch some fish, and a few attentive students master the casting technique quickly.

But most of us put away that fly rod until the next fishing trip, which may be months away, and learned lessons—casting stroke, timing and narrow loops—dissolve into a hazy memory. "Geez, did Bob tell me to stop the rod here or there? Thumb on top of the grip. Right? Do I cast with my wrist?" Forgotten lessons.

The answer is practice. This holds true for some veteran fly fishermen, most intermediate anglers and all novice fly casters.

*Practice. Practice. Practice.*

It's natural that after you've learned to cast you want to go fishing. You don't want to practice. Practice is boring, you say. It's like having to practice music scales when instead you want to play Bach or Beethoven. Or Brubeck or Basie.

My mission is to make "practice casting" so interesting that **you'll want to practice often.** Whenever you have some spare time.

Down the line you might even consider tournament casting. You don't have to compete in tournaments (although some of you may want to later on when those competitive juices start flowing). I'm talking about making casting practice so much fun, so challenging, that you not only develop good casting skills (so the next time you can make that cast to that enormous brown on a Montana stream or reach that tarpon on the flats), but actually *look forward* to your next session with enthusiasm.

What is great, is that you can do your target and distance casting practice almost anywhere, and it will only cost you a few dollars total. Every time you stop to sock a bucket of golf balls it costs money. Every time you shoot a round of trap or skeet it costs money. Right?

Not so in casting. In addition to the tackle that you probably already own, the practice casting materials will cost you about $15. Less if you want to make them yourself.

Remember: Much of the fun of fly fishing for trout is the actual fly casting. I once computed that, at our small fishing club, we made an average of 187 casts per person per rise (most of our fishing is "blind"). Doesn't it make sense then that you should enjoy your fly casting while fishing to a point where it is almost a reward in itself? The more you become skilled at fly casting, the more you're going to enjoy fly fishing.

**And catch more fish!**

*Peter Aravosis "made the cast" to catch this fine rainbow. You, too, will be able to make the cast, if you practice these events.*

# Where do we practice: ground or water?

THAT'S THE ADVANTAGE of fly-casting practice and games. You can do it anywhere. If you have a back yard that's about 80 to 100 feet of cleared space, you can do it there. Or maybe you live near a park. Or near an athletic field.

The advantage of casting on ground is that it's easy to place the targets and pick them up after practice and, later, when we tackle distance casting, it's easy to measure your casts. The disadvantage of casting on ground is that it is difficult to practice some casts (e.g., roll cast) because you need the pull or resistance of water on your fly line.

If you have access to a pond or a swimming pool, that's even better because casting on water simulates fishing conditions. The disadvantage of casting on water is placing and picking up the targets for the practice session and the necessity to anchor them so that they do not float away from wind, current or waves. It is also more difficult to measure your distance casts on water than on ground. Of course, you may be able to leave the targets in the water for extended periods of time, or maybe even start a casting club where the targets remain more or less permanently in the water (we'll discuss how to start a casting club in a later chapter).

If you live in the northern climes, a gymnasium is a wonderful place in the wintertime to sharpen your casting. If there are other anglers in your area who would or could be interested, most park districts or health clubs may welcome the formation of a casting club as an added activity.

That's the best part of practice casting.

*You can do it anywhere!*

# The targets and distance markers

**W**HEN WE WERE KIDS we wanted to learn how to throw a ball, rock, stick or snowball and, after we acquired the throwing motion, we wanted to see how accurate we could be and, finally, how far we could throw. We threw at objects. A garbage can. A tree. Whatever. And, boy, did we feel good when we hit our target! Right? Or when we could throw farther than the kid next door.

The same applies with casting. After we develop a casting stroke, and are comfortable with it, we need targets to practice our accuracy and markers to measure our distance.

Again, this book assumes that you learned the basic casting stroke. *Back cast, pause, forward cast. Back cast, pause, forward cast.* Once we learn the basics, there's nothing more boring than to cast on a lawn without a specific target or distance in mind.

So we need some targets. Here are some choices:

1) Brightly colored Hula Hoops make wonderful targets on the ground. I bought six for $14.87 at a "dollar"

## MAKE YOUR OWN TARGETS

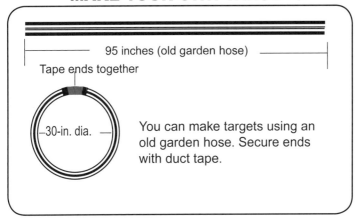

95 inches (old garden hose)

Tape ends together

30-in. dia.

You can make targets using an old garden hose. Secure ends with duct tape.

bargain store (and I think that the price even included an ice cream bar).

2) If you can't find Hula Hoops you can make your own targets from a variety of materials. An old brightly colored rubber hose is ideal. Make six hoops that are about 30 inches in diameter. Use duct tape to secure the ends together. You'll need about 95 inches of hose for each 30-inch target (30 in. X 3.1416 [*Pi*]).

3) If you are going to cast on water, you can use Hula Hoops or garden hose targets but you will have to use some pieces of wood, cork or other buoyant material to float them. You will also need some small weights and string to anchor the targets and to prevent them from drifting away.

Many casting clubs use water-tight aluminum targets but these are generally custom made by metal fabricators and tend to be expensive.

For the distance fly casting events, you have several options for measuring and marking devices:

1) You can obtain measuring tapes from various hardware or home improvement stores. These tapes have capacities of 100, 150 and 200 feet. (If you need more than that, why aren't you

competing in the National or World Casting Championships?)

2) If you prefer, you can make a simple distance measuring device. Take an old fishing reel with a capacity of about 200 feet of 20-pound monofilament or casting line. Carefully measure out 75 feet and tie on a small piece of colored yarn with a loop knot at that spot. Then measure out another 25 feet (the 100-foot mark) and put a different color yarn there. Do this again at 125 feet. If you feel very confident and are a very skilled caster, tie one on at 150 feet! Good for you!

3) Although not necessary, you'll find it helpful to use three small (12-inch) orange traffic cones. Place these at various distances (e.g., 75, 100, 125 feet to start). These safety cones make it easier for you to gauge the distance of your casts.

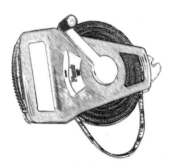

*A tape measure is a handy item for measuring distances . . . especially when you start making those astronomical casts!*

# Before we begin . . .

IN ADDITION to obtaining the targets and selecting a place to cast, you will of course need a fly rod, fly reel, matching line, leader, practice flies and a few other items. Let's quickly review:

**FLY ROD:** If you acquired a fly rod, you probably bought it based on the type of fishing you would do. If you are fishing for trout or panfish, it will be on the lighter, shorter side, taking a No. 5 or 6 line. If you plan to fish for bigger game (e.g., salmon, steelhead, pike, etc.,) it will be a longer rod (8½ feet) for a No. 8 or 9 line. For bonefish and small tarpon, a 9 ft. rod for a No. 8, 9 or 10 line would be a good outfit. These are, of course, approximate designations and your choice ultimately will reflect the waters you plan to fish. **Recommendation:** *Rely on the suggestions of an experienced angler or fly shop personnel. Don't buy first, and ask later!*

Nearly any length and size fly rod with perhaps some adjustment will work for many of the games in this book. If you are using, for example, a 7-ft. fly rod for a 4-weight line, move the targets closer to you (five or more feet), because there is a limitation as to how far anyone can cast with a very light fly rod. The ideal fly rod for most of these events would be 8½ to 9 feet in length and calibrated for No. 6, 7, or 8 fly lines.

**FLY REEL:** This is easy. Just about any fly reel will be suitable for these events as long as it has sufficient capacity to hold your fly line comfortably and is not extremely heavy.

**FLY LINE:** Again, the type of fly line depends on your fishing plans. Both double taper and weight forward lines can be used for these events as long as they match the fly-rod designation.

**PRACTICE LEADERS:** This is very important. Do not practice casting without a suitable leader (and practice fly) attached to your fly line. Start with a 7½-ft. leader, tapered to 3X for most of the events. You will need heavier leaders for some of the disciplines that dictate casting a big fly, but I'll guide you during those events.

**PRACTICE FLY:** It is equally important to tie on a practice fly even while executing a simple casting stroke. The leader and fly are as important to casting as a tail is to flying a kite.

You can tie on a piece of brightly colored yarn if you like. Trim it so that it's about ½-inch long and not overly fluffy.

*Best Bet:* Tie on a No. 10 or 12 bright fishing fly but be sure to remove the hook barb and point at the bend. If you are a fly tier, tie some flies similar to what is used in tournaments (see page 209). If you expect to fish for pike, bass and some salt water species, you'll need a few cork poppers (again remove the point and barb at the bend of the hook).

**EYE GLASSES:** Even though you will be practicing without a hook, be sure to wear sunglasses, prescription glasses, or plain eyeglasses whenever you are fly casting to protect your eyes from errant casts. That piece of yarn, practice fly and fly line can reach tremendous speeds and an errant cast can cause severe damage to unprotected eyes. **This is a must, whether you are practicing casting or actually fishing.**

**KEEP SCORE:** Would golf, bowling or other sports be popular activities if scores weren't kept? Of course not! It's important to keep casting scores so that you can accurately gauge your progress through practice. As you achieve higher scores, your success will serve as an incentive to practice more (see page 212).

**GET OTHERS INVOLVED:** You can practice these games on your own, but you might find it even more interesting if you involve your fishing friends, family or club members. If there are several fishing clubs around, you can easily hold tournaments at the various levels.

*Charles B. Mitchell, renowned wildlife artist, landed this salmon at a heavily fished Wisconsin river.*
*Charles is a very accomplished tournament caster. "I got into it years ago because I knew it would help my fishing."*

# And just a few more things . . .

WE'RE ALMOST READY to begin our lessons. Oops, I mean our games (after all, fly casting is fun!), but we need to establish a glossary or terminology of just a few words or phrases. Please be patient.

**MEASURING CAST:** In the first few lessons, we mention "measuring casts." This is simple. Nothing to it. They are merely casts to lengthen your line out to a target (usually the closest one). They are a novice's friend because they are "free," in that they are not counted toward your score.

**PRESENTATION CASTS:** Okay, these count for your score. The reason we count them, and keep score, is because it will help you gauge your progress. Furthermore, it will tell you when you are ready to advance to the next level (again, please stay on a level until you gain proficiency and confidence). Also known as "scored casts."

Another reason we have presentation (or scored) casts is that if you have a friendly competition with fishing pals, it's a way to determine the winner. And, later you may even want to enter more formal tournaments.

**FALSE CASTS:** These are casts that are aimed above water or ground so that they do not strike the surface and are used for four reasons: (1) to lengthen your cast, (2) to shorten your casts, (3) to gauge the distance of your cast, and (4) because it's "cool" to have your line traveling to and fro, in narrow undulating loops . . . and when you learn to do it, well, it's almost poetic.

***That's it. Let the games begin!***

# The three classifications of casting

I'VE DIVIDED the 11 levels of progressive casting in Section One into three classes: Merit, Expert and Masters (the terms are based on an old "Skish" tournament casting terminology). As you improve and progress from level to level, you also ascend to higher casting plateaus. When we learn something new, we need to measure our progress and feel a sense of accomplishment as we soar to higher elevations. Here are the three classifications, and briefly what is learned at each level.

## LEVEL 1-3

### *Merit Class*

IN MERIT CLASSIFICATION:

*Level One* hones in on the basic back cast, pause, forward cast and simple false casting.

*Level Two* concentrates on shooting more line on false casts.

*Level Three* will help improve your accuracy by making the same casting motion at specific distances.

**NOTE:** Don't rush it. Move from level to level only when you feel you've developed dexterity, confidence and accuracy. Think of the first three levels like a foundation in building a home.

## LEVEL **4-6**
### *Expert Class*

IN EXPERT CLASSIFICATION:

*Level Four* concentrates on accuracy and reduces the number of false casts and eliminates measuring casts.

*Level Five* teaches you to strip in line while false casting with your left hand (if you are a right-handed caster).

*Level Six* is a zig-zag exercise, in which you learn to change directions quickly and hit the targets with precision.

## LEVEL **7-11**
### *Masters Class*

IN MASTERS CLASSIFICATION:

*Level Seven* instructs you to deliver a fly very fast and accurately while extending and shortening line in a timed event!

*Level Eight* teaches you (1) to cast horizontally and, (2) over the opposite shoulder (so vital when the wind is blowing from the "wrong" direction).

*Level Nine* is a great discipline for casting big flies quickly and being able to change directions fast.

*Level Ten* is a distance fly-casting discipline . . . for those times when your normal cast is a few feet short of the target.

*Level Eleven* is a combination distance/accuracy fly-casting discipline . . . for those who demand a challenge!

# LEVEL**ONE**
## *Merit Class*

**TARGETS:** Place targets (A, B, C, D and E) approximately 20, 25, 30, 35 and 40 feet from the casting box as per diagram.

## Round One

Set up your fly rod, and attach a leader (about 7½ feet) and a practice fly.

1. Lengthen your cast by stripping a few feet of line from your reel until you hit Target A. Make as many casts on the ground or water as required to reach Target A. This a "measuring" cast and isn't scored. From here on the presentation casts count and are scored. Are you ready? Now lift up for your back cast and WITHOUT making any false casts, make a presentation cast to Target A (20 ft.), which counts as a scored cast. If you hit it, great! Congratulations!

2. If you miss it, just continue with the rest of the targets. Strip about five feet of line from your reel, make your back cast, pause for an instant and then make your presentation cast to Target B without any false casts in between.

3. Continue to the other targets: Strip about five feet of line, lift, back cast and make your presentation casts to Targets C, D and E.

Nice going!

Don't worry if you miss the targets. What's important right now is that you develop a rhythmic casting stroke: back cast, pause and forward cast. *Back cast, pause, forward cast.*

# LEVEL**ONE**
## *Merit Class*

40 ft.

35 ft.

30 ft.

25 ft.

20 ft.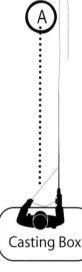

Casting Box

### QUICK START

1. Make a measurement cast (dotted line) to Target A .

2. Lift up and make your first presentation cast to Target A, which counts.

3. Strip about five feet of line from your reel and make your second presentation cast to Target B and then C, D and E without false casts.

4. In Round Two you will make two false casts between targets.

This is essential. It's the building block or foundation for future casting success. Keep practicing Round One until you consistently hit three out of the five targets and come within a few feet of the missed targets. Don't worry if it takes some time to acquire accuracy, especially on the distant targets. You can do it. I know you can!

**YOU WILL LEARN:** (1) That it is really a simple, rhythmic cast (be sure to accelerate before coming to a pause on both the back and forward casts); (2) That the line follows the arc of a rod tip; (3) That a fairly straight back and forward cast will deliver the fly in a reasonably straight path to the target; (4) That the longer the cast, the longer you must wait for the back cast to straighten out behind you before beginning your forward cast; (5) That it's important to shoot the line smoothly on the forward cast as you advance from target to target.

**IMPORTANT:** Please, please do not proceed to Round Two until you master Round One and you are very confident that you can hit the majority of targets most of the time. I know I'm being repetitive, but that's because it's important to develop your stroke and accuracy. Don't get discouraged.

## Round Two

Okay! Okay! You've developed confidence in your stroke and accuracy to the point you could almost do it with your eyes shut, and you know that you are ready to advance to the next level.

1. Again lengthen your measuring cast until you hit Target A (this cast isn't scored). Lift up and make two false casts and make your presentation (scoring) cast to Target A (20 ft.).

2. Strip about five feet of line off your reel. Lift the fly, make two false casts before delivering your presentation cast to Target B (25 ft.).

3. Repeat the same thing (strip, lift, two false casts, and presentation cast) to Targets C, D and E. See, it's easy.

Practice this until you are able to hit at least three targets most of the time and any misses are within a couple of feet from the target. Avoid hitting the ground or water during false casting (this is known as a "tick").

**YOU WILL LEARN:** (1) To develop and improve your false casting; (2) To deliver a more accurate cast; (3) To lengthen your casts by shooting line on the forward casts; (4) To avoid "ticking" the water/ground in front of you during false casting, which could scare off some fish or hamper your casting; (5) To develop a smooth rhythmic casting stroke so that it becomes second nature.

**TARGET CASTING ORDER:** A, B, C, D, E (both rounds).

**YOU'LL IMPROVE FASTER IF YOU:** Learn to throw a narrow loop on your back and forward casts. Narrow-loop casting is the most important component of accurate and distance casting. This is best accomplished (1) by accelerating your rod stroke before you come to an abrupt stop on the back cast or the forward cast; (2) by making sure that your rod travels in one plane; (3) by understanding that the line will follow the arc of the rod tip. You can read casting books, view tapes, listen to advice from experts, and in the end, it's something that you learn by trial and error. Keep experimenting with your stroke, and soon enough, you will see narrow loops unrolling. Suggestion: Check out the "Improve your casting with video!" chapter (page 130).

If you are hitting the water/ground in front of you during false casting, aim your false casts higher or begin the start of your back cast slightly faster. If the fly lands fairly close (within a few feet) to missed targets, you're on the right track. Just practice, practice and practice.

**TRY TO AVOID:** While there is a definite pause on the back cast, this pause should not be too long because the line will drop behind you and touch the ground or water. Yes, these two rounds may be a little tedious, but they are the foundation for all the other casting disciplines and events, and the lessons learned are absolutely necessary for successful fishing. *Tip:* After you gain some dexterity, you may find it helpful if you turn your head around (toward your casting arm) to observe the fly line on the back cast. Turn just your head and not your body, because that would change the path of the rod.

**AND REMEMBER:** The fly-casting motion is accomplished at three different fulcrums: the wrist, elbow and shoulder joints. Many beginners, especially those who have done a lot of spinning and plug casting, use their wrists too much if not almost entirely. For most fly casting, the elbow joint is mainly used.

**ASIDE:** I asked Chris Korich, one of the all-time best casters, what was the single most important element in successful casting. *"Easy. It's the casting loop,"* he responded immediately. *"Everything in fly casting is dependent on the loop. I don't care whether it is accuracy or distance fly casting . . . the loop is the most important element. Regardless of skill, the fly caster must always pay attention to the loop. It cannot be over-emphasized."*

**SCORING:** Give yourself ten points for every target you hit in each of the two rounds. Try to avoid "ticks," which is when your fly ticks the ground or water in front of you during false casting in Round Two. Starting in Level Three there will be two demerits for each tick.

**SAMPLE SCORING:** Let's say in Round One, you hit the first two targets (A & B), missed the third (C), made the fourth (D) and missed the fifth (E). You have a score of 30 for Round One. On Round Two, you hit targets A, C and D. You've hit a total of six targets out of ten for a score of 60.

**QUALIFICATION FOR MERIT LEVEL 1:** 60 points. If you do this on a fairly consistent basis, you're ready for the next level. If not, please, please, I beg you, keep practicing Level One. Some of the world's best casters started out very poorly.

# LEVEL**TWO**
## *Merit Class*

40 ft.

35 ft.

30 ft.

25 ft.

20 ft.

**QUICK START**

1. The same as Level One but this time you will practice your false casting. Dotted line is measurement (non-scoring) cast.

2. In Round One you make three false casts between the targets.

3. In Round Two you advance from target to target with two false casts.

4. You will learn to shoot line on your forward casts when it's necessary to lengthen your casts.

Casting Box

# LEVEL**TWO**
## *Merit Class*

**TARGETS:** Place targets (A, B, C, D and E) approximately 20, 25, 30, 35 and 40 feet from the casting box (same as Level One).

## Round One

1. Lengthen your cast until you hit the Target A (20 ft.) in a measuring, non-scoring cast. Lift up and make three false casts, and deliver your first presentation (scoring) cast to the same Target A.

2. Strip about ten feet of line from your reel. Lift the fly to start your back cast, make three false casts (letting out a little line on each forward cast) and then cast to Target C (30 ft.).

3. Strip about ten feet of line from your reel, lift up, make three false casts and deliver the fly to Target E (40 ft.).

4. Now strip in line (on the ground or water) from Target E until it's about the middle of Target B. Lift up, make three false casts and make your presentation cast to Target B (25 ft.).

5. Lift up, make three false casts and then deliver your presentation cast to Target D (35 ft.). Wow! Not that easy, huh. Keep practicing it. It takes time and patience to learn how to lengthen your cast by releasing line on the forward false casts.

**YOU WILL LEARN:** (1) To control the amount of line you shoot through the guides with your left hand; (2) To shoot

10 feet of line, by letting out a few feet on each of your three false casts and final presentation cast; (3) That shooting line on the longer targets (e.g., from Target C to E) may be easier than on the shorter targets (Target A to C) because the rod loads faster with the longer line.

**REMEMBER:** Pay attention to your casting loops. You want to develop a narrow, driving loop. At this stage of your casting development, the narrow loop is more important than hitting the targets. As you develop the loop you will gain line control and accuracy will be forthcoming.

**IMPORTANT:** Do **not** proceed to Round Two until you master Round One and gain confidence and skill to hit the majority of targets most of the time.

## Round Two

Exactly the same as Round One, but with only two false casts between targets instead of three. Yeah, it's harder, but you can do it with a little practice.

**TARGET CASTING ORDER:** A, C, E. Then B, D. (Both rounds.)

**YOU WILL LEARN:** (1) That advancing from Target A (20 ft.) to C (30 ft.) isn't easy, because there isn't enough line out to load the rod quickly. (2) That the medium and long casts may be easier.

**YOU'LL IMPROVE FASTER:** If, when lifting the line from the ground or water, you also use your left hand (if you are a right-handed caster) to increase line speed. Here's how: With your thumb and index finger of your left hand, grab the line near the first rod guide (stripper guide). As you begin the rod motion for your back cast, simultaneously pull the line with your left hand, which will increase line speed (this is known as a single haul). As you develop a strong back cast, you may find it easier to shoot a few feet of line on the back cast when needed as well as the forward cast. But for now shoot most of the line on the forward cast.

**SCORING:** 10 points a target (100 for perfect score).

**SAMPLE SCORING:** Let's say you hit Targets A, B, D and E in the First Round. That's 40 points you've earned. Let's assume you hit targets A, C and D in the second round. That's another 30 points for a total of 70 points! Great!

*Use your left hand to increase line speed and to load the rod quickly.*

**QUALIFICATION FOR MERIT LEVEL 2:** 60 points. (Fly should land within a couple of feet of missed targets).

*NOTE:* If you are using a very light fly rod, move the targets in five (or more feet) for this and other events.

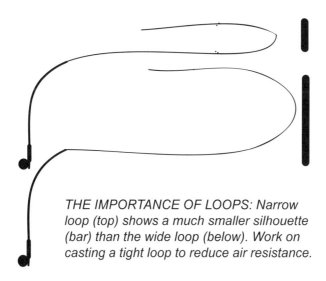

*THE IMPORTANCE OF LOOPS: Narrow loop (top) shows a much smaller silhouette (bar) than the wide loop (below). Work on casting a tight loop to reduce air resistance.*

# LEVEL**THREE**
## *Merit Class*

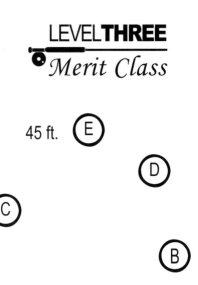

45 ft. **E**

**D**

**C**

**B**

**A** 25 ft.

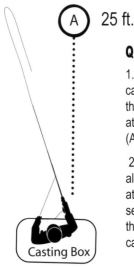

Casting Box

## QUICK START

1. After measuring cast (dotted line), make three presentation casts at each target (A, B, C, D and E).

2. Three false casts allowed on first presentation cast, two on the second, and only one on the third presentation cast.

# LEVEL**THREE**
## *Merit Class*

**TARGETS:** Place targets approximately 25, 30, 35, 40 and 45 feet away from the casting box. The closest (Target A) at 25 feet and the farthest (Target E) at 45 feet are directly in front of the box, the other three (B, C and D) are scattered as indicated in the diagram.

**PROCEDURE:** Start with just a few feet of line, plus leader and fly beyond the rod tip.

1. Lengthen your cast (by false casting) until you hit Target A (25 ft.) in a measuring, non-scoring cast.

2. Lift up, make no more than three false casts and then make a (scoring) presentation cast to Target A. Again lift up, make no more than two false casts and aim for the same target. Lift up, make one false cast for your third presentation cast to Target A.

3. Lift the fly, and using the same procedure advance to Target B. Obviously you will have to strip line from the reel while false casting to reach the target. Remember, no more than three false casts on the first presentation cast; two or less false casts on the second presentation cast; and one false cast on the third cast.

4. Repeat this procedure at Targets C, D and E.

**PENALTY:** Now we're going to add a penalty. If the fly strikes the water/ground while false casting, we deduct two points from your score. This is known as a tick. I know that seems harsh, but you're going to be an expert caster, right?

It's not that I had a bad morning (yeah, the Chicago Bears lost another game yesterday), so I'm taking it out on you. Here's the reasoning: You are fishing for spooky brown trout in a stream that's had considerable fishing pressure. You spot this trout, say within 40 feet of you. Nice fish! (By the way, aren't Polaroid glasses wonderful?) You know you can easily reach this fish because you've been practicing (and mastering!) the previous levels. No sweat! You even giggle, because you're so confident of your cast. So you make a few false casts, but one of the casts strikes the water in front of you. *ZOOM!* The trout is gone. *Darn!* (Or whatever expletive you prefer to use in such circumstances). That's why it is important not to hit the water (or ground) in practice during your false casting and every discernible tick means a deduction of two points.

**TARGET CASTING ORDER:** A, B, C, D and E.

**YOU WILL LEARN:** (1) That the first cast is very important, not only for a high score in this event, but in actual fishing: It's usually the <u>first</u> good presentation cast to a sighted trout that will (or won't) produce a rise; (2) To strip line from your reel and shoot it as you advance from target to target; (3) To avoid ticking or striking the water/ground in front of you while false casting; (4) To develop muscle memory and eye/hand coordination as you adjust your casts, so vital to fishing success.

**SCORING:** 10 points for the first presentation at each target; 6 points for the second presentation and 4 points for the third cast. Perfect Score: 100.

**SAMPLE SCORING:** Let's assume you hit Target A on the first and third casts (14 points); Target B on the second and third casts (10 points); Target C on the first cast (10 points); Target D on the second cast (6 points); Target E on first cast (10 points). Total points: 50. Nice round! Keep practicing! You're on your way to becoming a good caster.

**QUALIFICATION FOR MERIT LEVEL 3:** 60 points.

**GRADUATION TIME:** You practiced Levels One, Two and Three and most of you've made the qualifying scores several times. Congratulations! Well done! You're on your way! Treat yourself to something good. Maybe a triple scoop ice-cream sundae with hot fudge and all the trimmings (I say this because I'm an ice cream freak and on a diet).

Okay, some of you out there didn't make the qualifying scores. Yet. Not consistently, anyway. And a few didn't count all the ticks and didn't deduct the penalty points. *Tsk. Tsk.* Don't worry about it. Keep casting. Some of the world's best casters started out casting poorly. But they stayed with it. Today, they are world champs. Steve Rajeff is a good example. He started fly casting as a youngster and was having a terrible time with it. But he practiced and practiced and very shortly became a champion caster. He won the National all-round title 31 times and the biannual World Casting Championship 13 times in 17 tournaments. Besides being possibly the best caster of all time, he is among the very best all-round light tackle anglers today.

Keep practicing.

*And remember Rajeff!*

*Today's newcomer to fly casting is fortunate. There are dozens of excellent casting books, videos and Web sites. Forgot some of the casting strokes? This media is invaluable. Use it!*

# LEVEL**FOUR**

## *Expert Class*

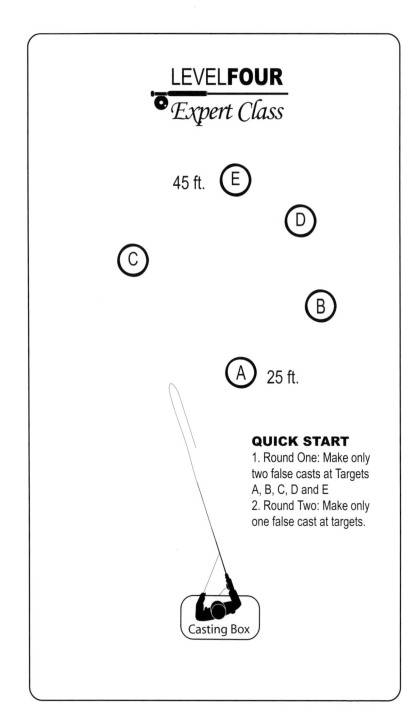

45 ft. (E)

(D)

(C)

(B)

(A) 25 ft.

**QUICK START**
1. Round One: Make only two false casts at Targets A, B, C, D and E
2. Round Two: Make only one false cast at targets.

Casting Box

# LEVEL**FOUR**
## *Expert Class*

**TARGETS:** Same as Level Three. Place targets approximately 25, 30, 35, 40 and 45 feet away from the casting box. The closest, Target A, at 25 feet and the farthest, Target E, at 45 feet are directly in front of the box, whereas the other three (B, C and D) are scattered as indicated in the diagram.

## Round One

As usual, start with a couple feet of fly line, leader and practice fly beyond the rod tip, and begin false casting.

1. Extend the line by stripping it from the reel and shooting it on the forward cast until you have reached Target A. Remember, the fly must not hit the ground/water during the false casts. When you think you have enough line to reach the first target, make your presentation cast, which is scored. You hit the first target? Good! Way to go.

*NOTE: There are no measuring casts as in the previous levels. Why? Well, if you were fishing for elusive, wary species (e.g., brown trout, bonefish and permit) making casts on the water to reach the necessary distance would spook the fish. So we must learn to lengthen our line by false casting in the air. In effect, false casting accomplishes the same as measuring casts except that we are casting in the air and not on the surface. We learn to judge the distances while the fly is in motion in front of us.*

2. Now lift up, make no more than two false casts and aim for Target B. Of course, while false casting, you will have to strip sufficient line from the reel to reach the target, but

you learned this in earlier lessons, so you shouldn't have any trouble doing it. Right?

3. Lift up again, make no more than two false casts and then a presentation cast to Target C. Continue to Targets D and E. *Remember, no more than two false casts between targets.* If the fly strikes the water/ground while false casting you are charged two demerits per tick, so be careful.

**TARGET CASTING ORDER:** A, B, C, D and E.

## Round Two

Reel in line so that you have only a couple feet of fly line, leader and fly beyond the rod tip.

1. False cast as many times as you like and make your presentation (scored) cast to Target A.

2. Repeat the same procedure as Round One but with only one false cast between targets. Sure, it's getting a little harder, but, hey, you're getting better. Right?

**YOU WILL LEARN:** (1) To lengthen or shorten your line by false casting in the air, without hitting the water/ground in front of you; (2) To strip line from your reel and to shoot it on forward casts; (3) To judge distances between targets while adjusting the right amount of line; (4) To develop eye/hand coordination to a point that it becomes second nature; (5) To make faster, but accurate deliveries, especially as required in Round Two.

**YOU'LL IMPROVE FASTER IF:** You concentrate on throwing a narrow loop on both the back and forward casts. Narrow loops will increase your accuracy and make fly casting a wonderful, relaxing activity. I'm going to mention the narrow loops often throughout these lessons because they are most important. Remember what Chris Korich said about loops in Level One? The narrow, controlled loops are the most important part in successful distance and accuracy fly casting.

**TIP:** You might want to experiment with releasing a little line on the back cast during false casts but shoot the majority of the line on the forward (false or presentation) casts. This is particularly important in the shorter distances (as when advancing from Target A to Target B) because it is harder to "load the rod" with the shorter amount of line out. Try it and decide for yourself whether you prefer it. Shoot line on back casts only when necessary. Most casters do not shoot line on the back cast.

**SCORING:** 10 points for every hit. Perfect Score: 100

**SAMPLE SCORING:** Let's say you hit Targets A, C, D and E in the First Round but only target C and D in the Second Round. That's six targets at 10 points each, for a total of 60 points. Nice rounds!

**QUALIFICATION FOR EXPERT LEVEL 4:** 60 points and coming close on missed targets.

*You are casting well enough to tackle trout on many streams. But don't stop now! Our goals are loftier. Keep going. If you continue to practice, you're going to be a superb caster . . . among the very best!*

# LEVEL**FIVE**
### *Expert Class*

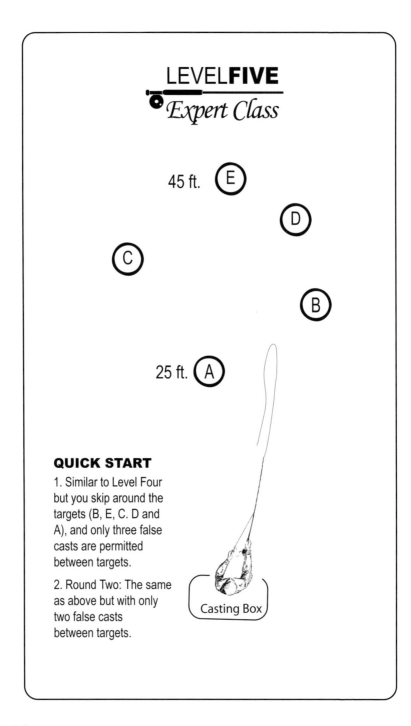

45 ft. (E)

(D)

(C)

(B)

25 ft. (A)

## QUICK START

1. Similar to Level Four but you skip around the targets (B, E, C. D and A), and only three false casts are permitted between targets.

2. Round Two: The same as above but with only two false casts between targets.

Casting Box

# LEVEL**FIVE**
## *Expert Class*

**TARGETS:** Place targets approximately 25, 30, 35, 40 and 45 feet away from the casting box. The closest, Target A, at 25 feet and the farthest, Target E, at 45 feet are directly in front of the box, whereas the other three (B, C and D) are randomly scattered as indicated in the diagram.

## Round One

Hold the practice fly in your left hand (if you are a right-handed caster) and begin to false cast.

1. Strip and shoot enough line until you think the fly is over Target B (30 feet) and then deliver your first presentation cast (which is scored).

2. Lift up, make three false casts, stripping line from your reel, and make a presentation cast to Target E (45 ft.).

3. Lift the fly, make three false casts and then proceed to Target C (35 ft.). Note: To go from a distant target (E) to a closer target (C) you will have to strip line in while false casting. Strip line in with your left hand while controlling the amount with your right index finger or middle finger against the rod handle (as per illustration on page 49).

4. After Target C, lift, make three false casts, (allowing sufficient line to shoot through the guides) and hit Target D (40 ft.).

5. Lift, make three false casts while stripping line in, and hit Target A (25 ft.). Whew! Yeah, I know, it's not easy but keep practicing until you get the hang of it. I know you will, *if*

*you practice.* And, of course, don't proceed to Round Two until you've developed the necessary confidence.

**TARGET SEQUENCE:** B, E, C, D and A.

# Round Two

Same as above but with only two false casts between targets. You should have little trouble in accomplishing this, if you've mastered Round One.

**YOU WILL LEARN:** (1) To strip out line from the reel and shoot it while false casting; (2) To strip line in (to shorten it) with your left hand (while false casting) using your right middle or index finger and rod handle to control the amount of line; (3) To develop and improve eye/brain/hand coordination and muscle memory as you gauge distances and adjust the line between targets.

**YOU'LL IMPROVE FASTER IF:** You practice, without actually casting, pulling line in with your left hand. Set up your fly outfit and pull out about 60 feet of line. Then hold the rod (don't cast), and with your left hand practice pulling the line under your middle or index finger of your casting hand. Pull about two to three feet of line at a time. Actually, you don't even need a rod, reel and line to practice this: you can pretend there is one in your hands. Keep practicing this, until you get the hang of it, then incorporate this into your casting.

**SCORING:** 10 points for every hit. Perfect Score: 100.

**SAMPLE SCORING:** Assume you hit Targets B and E in the First Round and Targets B and A in the Second Round. That's four targets at 10 points each, for a total of 40 points. Not bad. With a little practice, you will conquer this event! Keep it up!

**QUALIFICATION FOR EXPERT LEVEL 5:** 50 points (within a couple feet on missed targets).

# LEVEL**SIX**
## *Expert Class*

**TARGETS:** Place Targets A and B at approximately 25 feet from casting box but at about a 45-degree angle left and right. Place Targets C and D approximately 35 feet from casting box, also at a 45-degree angle. Target E is placed 45 feet from the casting box at a 45-degree angle to the right of the casting box.

## Round One

Again, start with a few feet of fly line, leader and practice fly beyond the rod tip.

1. Begin false casting and extending line, by stripping it from the reel and shooting it on the forward cast until you have reached Target A. Make your presentation cast.

2. Lift up, make two false casts and go to Target B.

3. Lift up, make two more false casts and switch to Target C.

4. Do the same for Target D and E. Where required, you will have to strip sufficient line from your reel during false casts as you progress from target to target.

## Round Two

1. Lift up from target E and begin false casting and stripping in line (while false casting—max five false casts) until you have retrieved sufficient line to hit Target A. Make your presentation cast to Target A.

2. Continue with the same procedure as in Round One, but this time allow only one false cast between targets.

# LEVEL**SIX**
## *Expert Class*

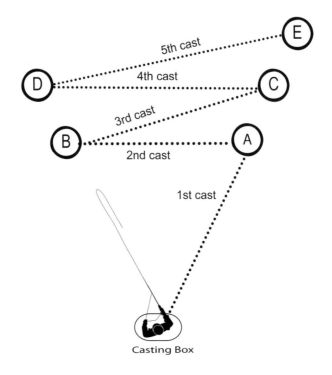

## QUICK START

1. Round One: After presentation cast to Target A, lift, make two false casts and deliver fly to Target B. Two more false casts and cast to Target C. Continue to Targets D and E (two false casts in between).

2. Round Two: Lift fly from Target E and **within 5 false casts** shorten your cast to hit Target A. Then repeat as in Round One but with only one false cast in between targets.

**TARGET SEQUENCE:** A, B, C, D and E (Both Rounds).

**YOU WILL LEARN:** (1) To switch directions quickly with a minimum of false casts. This is so important particularly when one is casting to rising fish, such as trout, or moving fish such as bonefish; (2) To strip and feed line through the guides while false casting; (3) The importance of line control in switching directions from target to target.

**SCORING:** 10 points for every hit. Perfect Score: 100.

**SAMPLE SCORING:** You deliver perfect casts to Targets C and E in Round One and Targets A and D in Round Two. That's four targets at 10 points each, for a total of 40 points. This is a very challenging event, but since you've been practicing, you've noted your improvement. Right? Of course!

**QUALIFICATION FOR EXPERT LEVEL 6:** 60 points.

**GRADUATION TIME!** If you are meeting the qualification scores for Level Six consistently, you're ready for Master Level events.

**CONGRATULATIONS!** You're on your way to becoming a superb caster. Keep it up. Pat yourself on your back, take a bow, relax a bit, and get ready for more casting fun!

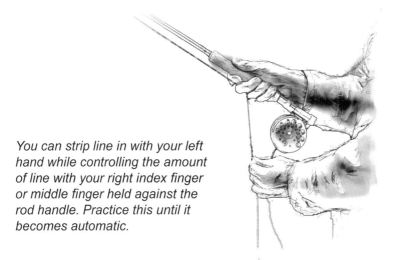

*You can strip line in with your left hand while controlling the amount of line with your right index finger or middle finger held against the rod handle. Practice this until it becomes automatic.*

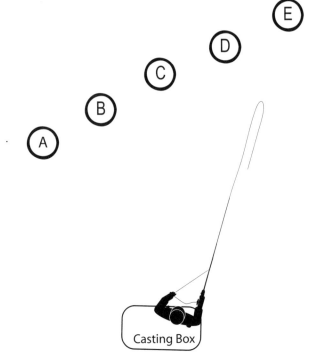

# LEVEL**SEVEN**
## *Masters Class*

### QUICK START

1. Round One: Make your presentation(s) cast to Target A. After you hit it, lift up and make at least one false cast and then advance to Target B. If you miss, make a false cast and continue until you hit it. Similarly progress to Targets C, D and E.

2. Round Two: Lift, false cast and go back to Target E, then D, C, B and A. You must adjust your line while false casting. One more thing: **You have one minute to make as many targets as you can.**

# LEVEL**SEVEN**

*Masters Class*

**TARGETS:** Place Target A about 25 feet from caster's box and to the left at a 30 to 45 degree angle. Place Target E about 45 feet away and at a 30 to 45 degree angle to the right of the box. The three other targets (B, C, and D) are placed equidistant at 30, 35 and 40 feet.

## Round One

Start with a few feet of fly line, leader and practice fly beyond the rod tip.

1. Begin false casting and extending the line, by stripping it from the reel and shooting it on the forward cast until you feel that you have reached Target A. Make your presentation cast to Target A. If you miss, keep casting to Target A until you hit it, **but you must make one false cast between presentation casts.**

2. When you hit the target, pick up, strip line from the reel, make one false cast, and deliver the fly to Target B. If you miss, keep casting until you hit the target.

3. Proceed to Targets C, D and E progressively. You must make one false cast between presentation casts.

**TARGET SEQUENCE:** A, B, C, D and E.

## Round Two

1. After you hit Target E, in Round One, lift up, make one false cast and again deliver the fly to E.

2. Pick up, make one false cast (stripping in line with left hand) and drop the fly into Target D.

3. Lift up and go to Targets C, B and A.

**TARGET SEQUENCE:** E, D, C, B and A.

**IMPORTANT:** This is a one-minute timed event! Time begins after first presentation to Target A. For a perfect score, you must hit all ten targets within one minute. Remember: You must hit a target before advancing to the next and you must make at least one false cast between presentation casts. If you hit all ten targets in less than a minute repeat Round One (and Two!) and earn bonus points.

**YOU WILL LEARN:** (1) How to make rapid-fire accurate casts (so important when casting to rising or fast-moving fish); (2) How to lengthen or shorten your line quickly while false casting; (3) That the constant line adjustments "on the fly" will vastly improve your eye/brain/hand coordination.

**TIP:** Because this is a **one-minute event**, have a friend time you, and, periodically, call out the remaining seconds. You'll be too busy making perfect casts to look at your watch. But what if no one's around? Use a cooking timing device. A good, inexpensive one is the battery powered West Bend 40005 digital, with an audio alarm (see illustration). Set it for one minute, and let the fun begin.

**SCORING:** 10 points for every hit. Perfect Score: 100. 10 Bonus points for every target you hit beyond 10 within the one-minute time limit. *Optional*: A demerit of two points for each tick.

**SAMPLE SCORING:** Since you can't advance from target to target until you hit them, it's easily scored. If you hit the first five targets you get 50 points. But let's say you hit all ten targets and you have 15 seconds left, so you hit Target A and B again. *Wow!* You have 120 points.

**QUALIFICATION FOR MASTERS LEVEL 7**: Minimum— 80 points (hit eight targets within one minute).

**ASIDE:** Looks easy, but it's a little fooler, and some very good casters have found this event challenging and even frustrating. This is a fast-moving event, because you not only have to hit the targets but you also have to beat the clock. It's a great event for various fishing clubs, looking for an exciting casting discipline for their picnics or get-togethers. But besides being fun, this event will be extremely helpful in your fishing because it teaches you to cast fast and accurately and to strip line out and in while false casting.

*My favorite accuracy event.*

# LEVEL**EIGHT**
## *Masters Class*

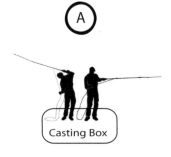

(A)

(D)    Casting Box    (B)

(C)

## QUICK START

1. Round One: All casts in this round are made horizontal (rod parallel to ground or water). Four false casts and presentation cast to Target A. Same with Targets B, C and D. Remember the rod must travel in a horizontal position.

2. Round Two: Same as Round One but casts must be made over the opposite shoulder. If right handed, rod travels over left shoulder (again as parallel to ground or water as possible). Leaning head and shoulders in that direction helps.

# LEVEL**EIGHT**
## *Masters Class*

**TARGETS:** Place four targets approximately 35 to 45 feet from caster's box at 0, 90, 180 and 270 degrees as per diagram. Target A is approximately at 35 feet, Target B at 45 feet, Target C at 35 feet and Target D at 45 feet.

## Round One

**All casts in this round are via side or horizontal casting (rod, line and leader travel horizontal to ground/water).**

Start with a few feet of fly line, leader and practice fly beyond the rod tip.

1. Begin horizontal false casting and extending line by stripping it from the reel and shooting it on the forward cast until you have reached Target A. Make no more than four horizontal false casts to each target plus your presentation cast.

2. Do the same for other targets, turning your body as you see fit to cast to each target. Make a fifth cast to Target A.

**YOU WILL LEARN:** (1) To cast accurately in a horizontal plane, which, among other advantages, allows you to place a fly under overhanging branches; (2) To change directions quickly while fishing; (3) To develop a very narrow loop because you can observe the back casts and forward casts easily; (4) An indispensable cast for windy conditions (usually there is less wind closer to the water); (5) A superb cast for heavy or bulky flies, because you are less likely to hit yourself with a horizontal cast than with a vertical cast.

# Round Two

The procedure is the same as Round One except that all casts are made over the **opposite** shoulder of your casting arm. If you are right handed, the rod tip, line, leader and fly travel over your left side.

1. After Round One, reel in so that you have just a few feet of line beyond the rod tip and begin false casting (max four false casts) over the opposite shoulder of your casting arm. The angle of this cast may be anywhere from almost vertical to almost horizontal, but again the rod tip and line, leader and fly travel over the opposite shoulder. Cast to Target A.

2. Proceed to Targets B, C, D and back to A. It will be necessary to turn your body to address the various targets.

**YOU WILL LEARN:** (1) An excellent cast when there is considerable wind from the right side of a right-handed caster (or left side from a left-handed caster). The wind blows the line, leader and fly away from the you, which reduces the chances of hooking yourself; (2) When fishing in a skiff or small craft with a partner, you can direct the line away from him/her. (3) A useful and safer cast when wading a stream with a companion or guide who is just to the right of you (if you are right handed). **Note:** If you practice this event in very windy conditions, adjust the target positions accordingly until you've mastered this event. As you gain confidence and skill, be sure to practice all these events on windy days, because often you will encounter unfavorable winds while fishing.

**TARGET SEQUENCE:** A, B, C, D, & A (both rounds, ten casts total).

**SCORING:** 10 points for every hit. Perfect Score: 100.

**SAMPLE SCORING:** You hit Targets A, B and D in Round One and Targets B and C in Round Two. That's five targets at 10 points each, for a total of 50 points. This is not an easy event but so crucial for many fishing applications. Take your time and practice it.

**QUALIFICATION FOR MASTERS LEVEL 8:** 70 points.

*Robert Tomes has taken more big muskies on a fly than anyone I know: "Fly fishing for muskies is not a high percentage sport; they're just not very plentiful on even the best waters and they are very wary. Fly casting for muskies is hard work. It requires a lot of energy and stamina . . . better get those casting muscles in shape before you give this very challenging sport a try!"*

# LEVEL**NINE**

## *Masters Class*

**TARGETS:** Place Targets A and C approximately 40 feet from caster's box and Targets B, E, and D are 60 feet from the box. Target E is directly in line with the Caster's Box. Targets A and C are approximately 12 feet apart. Targets B, E, and D are also placed 12 feet apart, as per diagram.

**NOTE:** This event is designed for casting bigger, bulkier flies, such as those used for permit, tarpon, snook and other saltwater species. It is also an ideal event for casting big poppers and larger, air-resistant flies for pike, muskies, bass and other freshwater species that may prefer bigger flies.

**EQUIPMENT:** Since you will be casting heavier flies and making longer distances, use a heavier outfit. An 8½- to 9-ft. rod that takes a No. 8 (or heavier) weight forward tapered line is ideal. Tie on a 7-ft. leader that tapers to 2X or 1X. Use flies similar to what you expect to use in fishing, but again snip off the point and barb at the bend for safety.

**REQUIRED:** Knowledge and execution of double haul.

## Round One

1. Strip about 70 feet from the reel. Spread it on the ground in loose, roughly three-foot loops. Begin false casting and make your presentation cast to Target A.

2. Pick up, make two false casts and deliver the fly to Target B.

3. Strip in line (on the water or ground) so that the fly is approximately at the 40-foot targets.

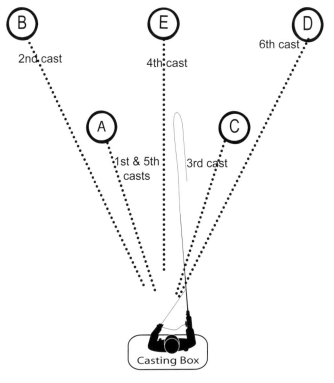

# LEVEL**NINE**
## *Masters Class*

**B** — 2nd cast

**E** — 4th cast

**D** — 6th cast

**A** — 1st & 5th casts

**C** — 3rd cast

Casting Box

## QUICK START

1. Round One: False cast and deliver presentation cast to Target A; then after two false casts make presentation cast to Target B. Strip in line and deliver presentation cast to Target C. Lift up, two false casts and presentation cast to Target E. Strip back to close targets and make another presentation cast to A. Lift up, two false casts and presentation cast to D.

2. Round Two: Same as Round One but with only one false cast instead of two. It isn't easy. So don't get discouraged!

4. Lift up, make two false casts and then a presentation cast to Target C.

5. Lift up, two false casts, and hit Target E.

6. Strip the line (on water or ground) back to 40-ft. mark, lift, two false casts, and cast again at Target A.

7. Lift up, two false casts and hit Target D.

## Round Two

Same as Round One but only **one false cast permitted between targets.**

**TARGET SEQUENCE:** A, B, C, D, A, E (Six casts total each round.)

**YOU WILL LEARN:** (1) The advantage of the double-haul casting technique, which is absolutely necessary for distance casting, e.g., going from the close targets (A and C) to the distant targets (B, E, D). Anyone fishing saltwater for permit, tarpon, bonefish and other species should practice this event using similar flies but remove the point and barb for safety reasons. This also applies to freshwater species that require bigger flies or poppers; (2) A great discipline for the experienced fly caster who wishes to perfect his double-haul technique and be able to deliver long, accurate casts.

**YOU'LL IMPROVE FASTER IF YOU:** Study and practice the double-haul technique (away from the targets) until you have developed a smooth motion. It is an essential technique for many saltwater and freshwater applications. After you've attained a fairly smooth double haul, practice this event. Don't try to do this discipline strictly with power and without the double haul.

**SCORING:** *In Round One:* Five points for any hits on the closer targets (A and C). Ten points for any hits on the distant targets (B, E and D) in the first round (where two false casts are allowed). *In Round Two:* Five points for any hits on

Targets A and C, and 15 points for any hits on the distant targets in the second round (where only one false cast is permitted). Perfect score: 105 points.

**SAMPLE SCORING:** This is a little tricky because of the different points assigned for distant vs. close targets. Let's say you hit Targets A (5 points), B (10 points) and E (10 points) in the Round One for a total of 25 points. In the Round Two you hit Targets A (5 points) and C (5 points) for a total of 10 points. Your total score is 25 (First Round) and 10 points (Second Round) for a total of 35 points.

**QUALIFICATION FOR MASTERS LEVEL 9: 60 points.**

**ASIDE:** Not an easy discipline (heck, it's tough enough figuring out the math for the score!), but what an essential

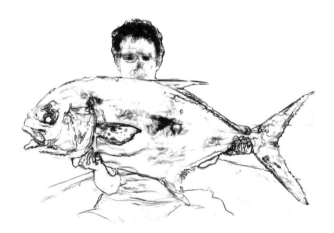

*Winston Moore is one of the world's most successful anglers for big permit on a fly. Winston caught this giant permit (displayed by his guide). It measured 51 inches in length and is undoubtedly the largest permit landed on a fly! After measuring and photographing the fish, Winston released it.*

*Winston is a powerful caster, master of the double haul and is a very accurate caster. "Anyone after big permit on a fly better practice his casting **before** the trip. Accuracy is important but so is distance."*

event for casting big flies. If your fishing requires throwing large, bulky flies, practice this event over and over again.

While the different changes in casting direction and distances may seem unnecessary, this is practically a cast-for-cast duplication of situations I've encountered numerous times while fishing for tarpon in Belize as well as for other species elsewhere. *It has many fishing applications.*

Don't forget, this is a Level Nine discipline, so it isn't easy. If you started out as a novice and made it this far, you've done a fantastic job.

Big time!

# LEVEL**TEN**
## *Masters Class*

**TARGETS:** None. But you'll need a long measuring line or tape. You can obtain a long measuring tape from a home building supply house or major hardware store, or make a measuring device from 20-pound monofilament or braided line. Wind it on an old fishing reel or spool for convenience. Tie in small pieces of different colored bright yarn at distances of 75, 100 and 125 feet to start. You can place bigger markers (hat, pieces of cloth, traffic cones, etc.) next to the yarn for better visibility from caster's box.

**REQUIRED:** Knowledge and ability to execute a smooth double haul **is absolutely necessary**.

**DISTANCE FLY-CASTING EVENT:** We're not concerned with extreme accuracy here, mostly with distance. I know I'm repeating myself, but you need to know and execute the basic double-haul technique and you need to be able to cast a narrow loop. If you aren't interested in very long casts, you don't have to bother with this event. But I'm going to tell you that once you get the hang of it, many of you will find it exhilarating—like booming a 50-yard field goal or hitting a golf ball 300 yards. *Whoa*, it's fun, especially as you begin to attain those long casting distances that defy the laws of physics and gravity.

**PROCEDURE:** You will need a lawn, park, or athletic field that has about 175 feet of cleared space to accommodate your back and presentation casts. You want a tail wind, but if only a side wind is available (because of trees or other obstacles),

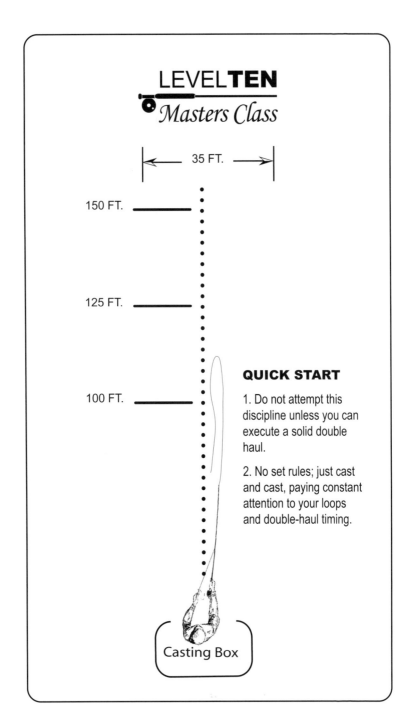

# LEVEL**TEN**

## *Masters Class*

← 35 FT. →

150 FT. ————

125 FT. ————

100 FT. ————

### QUICK START

1. Do not attempt this discipline unless you can execute a solid double haul.

2. No set rules; just cast and cast, paying constant attention to your loops and double-haul timing.

Casting Box

position yourself so that the wind blows from left to right if you're a right-handed caster.

Stretch out your measuring line to the maximum distance you feel you can cast. *Remember:* You may want to place larger markers, such as small traffic cones, at the various distances (next to the yarn) for better visibility.

This event is best cast with a longer, heavier rod, ideally 8½ to 9 feet calibrated to handle a No 7, or heavier, shooting head. Use a 7½ leader that tapers down to 2X or 1X. Tie on a very small piece of brightly colored yarn as your practice fly.

**Important:** Before you begin to cast, you should warm up for a few minutes: Perform some stretching exercises and move your outstretched arms in circles for a few minutes clockwise and then counterclockwise and finally swing them back and forth in front of you. Loosen up those muscles.

After a few, short warm-up casts, begin your distance casts down the measuring line/tape, paying particular attention to executing the double haul, throwing a narrow loop, and "accelerating to a sudden stop" on the back and forward casts. You'll probably find that two false casts prior to your presentation distance cast will work best. Timing, casting stroke and loop control are more important than brawn. Cast for five minutes at each session and then rest for about 10 minutes, or bad casting habits could develop. Do not cast more than three five-minute segments a day during your initial practice sessions.

During each session write down the distances of your three best casts on a scorecard. You can estimate the distances accurately (e.g., if your fly lands halfway between the 100- and 125-foot markers on your measuring line, then your cast is about 113 feet.) It's important to keep track of your distance casts so that you can note your progress, which will fire you up for future sessions.

**YOU WILL LEARN:** (1) To improve the double-haul technique, which is so vital in distance casting (remember, the double haul is also essential for casting bulky flies, particularly under windy conditions); (2) The importance of casting a narrow loop; (3) That the precise timing and blending of the double haul, stroke and trajectory are more important than brawn.

**EXTREME DISTANCES:** If you wish to attain extreme casting distances after you've perfected the double haul, use a fast-sinking shooting head (e.g., extra-fast sinking 38-ft. head) and about .015 in. monofilament for the running or shooting line. You'll be amazed! But learn and practice the double haul first until you can execute it perfectly!

**SCORING:** Measure your longest cast within the five-minute casting session.

## QUALIFICATION FOR MASTERS LEVEL 10:

*Using a standard weight forward line:*

| | |
|---|---|
| Five-weight outfit | 70 ft. plus |
| Six-weight outfit | 80 ft. plus |
| Seven- or eight-foot outfit | 90 ft. plus |

*Using a shooting head and monofilament backing (.015 in. diameter or heavier):*

| | |
|---|---|
| Five-weight outfit | 80 ft. plus |
| Six-weight outfit | 95 ft. plus |
| Seven- or eight-weight | 105 ft. plus |
| Heavier | 120 ft. plus |

**ASIDE:** Again, it's an exhilarating event that's excellent exercise, especially if you move up to the heavier lines (e.g., No. 9 or 10). It has some value in fishing but let's face it: The extreme distances are ego gratifying. With dedicated practice you'll be able to throw a fly about twice as far as anyone you probably know. (Unless you know Tim or Steve Rajeff, Henry Mittel, Chris Korich, Rene Gillibert and other superb distance casters).

# LEVEL**ELEVEN**

## Masters Class

SOME ANGLERS SNEER at the distance fly-casting events and tournaments: "What good is it if you can throw a fly a mile without any accuracy?" Good point! So here's a discipline that will satisfy the anglers who enjoy throwing the long line but also accurately. The best of both worlds!

**TARGET:** We're going to use six-foot targets for this game, and unless you know where "Bigfoot" or other giants buy their Hula Hoops, you're going to have to make your own. No problem.

See that old garden hose that you haven't used for years? Just cut off a large section to make a six-foot diameter, attach both ends with duct tape, and you're ready. You'll need about 19 feet of hose for each 6 ft. target (6 ft. X 3.1416 [*Pi*]).

If you don't want to bother with a hose, you could use just about anything else for a target. Example: Take an old bed sheet and fold it so that you have a 6 x 6 ft. target. It does not have to be a round target.

Using your measuring tape from the previous event, start by placing your six-foot target at 75 feet. If you are an extremely good caster, you could start at 100 feet. Hitting a 6-ft. target at 75 ft. is not an easy task, especially if you are using a lighter fly rod like a 5 or 6 wt.

**REQUIRED:** Again, ability to execute a smooth double haul **is absolutely necessary**.

**DISTANCE/ACCURACY FLY-CASTING EVENT:** To

# LEVEL**ELEVEN**
## *Masters Class*

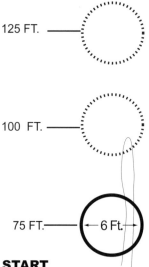

125 FT. ——

100 FT. ——

75 FT.—— 6 Ft.

## QUICK START

1. This event combines distance and accuracy. Start with close target before advancing to farther targets.

2. Best to practice with a partner. Three casts to targets. Closest cast determines winner.

Do not attempt this discipline unless you can execute a solid double haul.

Casting Box

begin, after a few warm-up exercises and some short casts, simply start casting at the target, paying attention to your loops, double haul, and, of course, accuracy. If you have trouble getting the distance, move the target in, but not too close! Remember this is a combined distance/accuracy event.

The best way to progress and to increase the enjoyment of this event is to find a friend with similar casting skills and take turns casting and judging. It's not easy to determine whether the fly hits the target or not, especially as you progress to the more distant targets. A judge or a spotter helps.

After you both practice a few times and get the hang of it, you can engage in friendly casting competition. Here's how to do it: Get a few of those wooden plant sticks (they are pointed, and about 8 x 2 inches and thin) from a garden shop to  mark the casts. Actually you can use any visible objects.

Take turns casting and judging. Start with the close target. If the caster hits the target, the judge yells PERFECT! Change over after  three casts. The caster who comes closest (or hits the target!) "wins," but think of this a team effort rather than competition (later in the book we'll provide you with many competitive events).

It's not only more fun casting with a friend or friends, but you can offer advice to each other for improvement, since it is very difficult for a caster to observe his/her casting technique.

After you have developed sufficient distance/accuracy for the close target, you can progress to the longer targets.

I've arbitrarily set the targets at 75, 100 and 125 feet, but they can set at any distance—either closer, or, if you are a terrific caster, farther.

**YOU WILL LEARN:** (1) To make longer, accurate casts. (2) The necessity of the double-haul casting technique, which is not only essential for distance but also vital for accuracy in longer casts. The double haul helps create a tighter loop and develop line speed.

**QUALIFICATION FOR MASTERS LEVEL 11:** None. You be your own judge!

*Stu Apte is considered one of the finest (if not the best) all-round anglers of all time. Although a savvy angler on all gamefish, Stu earned his lofty reputation as a tarpon guide and fisherman. "In fly fishing for tarpon, you not only need to be able to cast the fly accurately—often with long casts—but it is important to deliver it FAST! And be sure to practice casting in windy conditions before your tarpon trip. It's usually windy on the flats!"*

# SECTION TWO

OKAY, YOU'VE PRACTICED the "Levels" events and you have cast the qualifying scores with consistency. You have learned and mastered some of the advanced techniques.

You are ready for additional casting challenges. This section presents the American Casting Association (ACA) official fly events and rules.

The ACA is a federation of U. S. and Canadian angling and casting clubs. The association encourages groups and individuals to enjoy casting and angling as recreation and sport. It sponsors the ACA National Tournament each year at different cities and also coordinates regional casting tournaments held by individual clubs.

Competition includes fly and plug casting events in accuracy and distance. Many of the major tackle innovations and casting methods were developed by tournament casters.

The following fly events are not only fun and challenging, but they will also make you a better caster and a more successful angler.

Give them a try.

For more information on the ACA, including tournaments, tackle and tips, log on

*http://www.americancastingassoc.org*

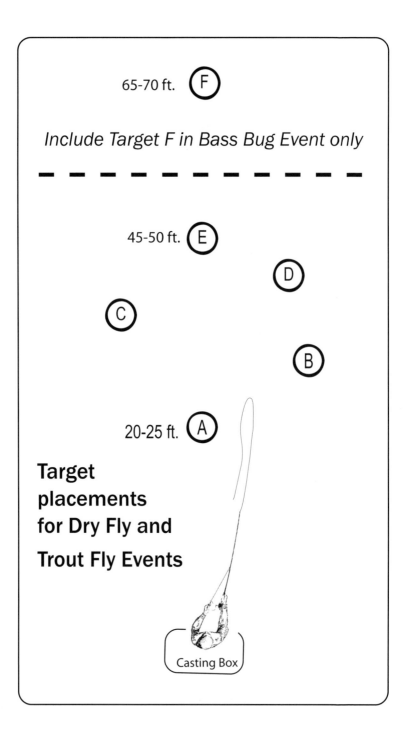

65-70 ft. Ⓕ

*Include Target F in Bass Bug Event only*

- - - - - - - - - - - - -

45-50 ft. Ⓔ

Ⓓ

Ⓒ

Ⓑ

20-25 ft. Ⓐ

**Target
placements
for Dry Fly and
Trout Fly Events**

Casting Box

# The Dry Fly Event

ONE OF THE MOST POPULAR tournament casting games is the classic Dry Fly Event. It's not only a springboard to successful trout fishing, but also it's very helpful in many other fly-fishing applications where casting accuracy is essential.

**TARGETS:** You'll need five Hula Hoops or 30-inch targets made from a brightly colored water hose and duct tape (see page 19). Place the nearest one between 20 to 25 feet from the caster's box and the farthest at 45 to 50 feet. **Important:** Measure the distances to the near and far targets (most of us tend to over-estimate distances). Place the other three targets randomly between the near and far targets, but not in a straight line. *See diagram.*

**THE TACKLE:** Just about any balanced fly tackle can be used for this event but here are some suggestions:

*Rod:* Like most sporting equipment there is no such thing as one size fits all. If you use a lighter, short fly rod (8 feet or less), you may have to bring in the targets about five or more feet. If you intend to compete in tournaments, you'll find it advantageous to use an 8½- or 9-ft. rod. The longer rods are particularly helpful in casting in windy conditions. The most popular outfit among most casters is a 9-ft. tip action fly rod that is calibrated for a 7-weight. On windy days many casters switch to an 8-weight outfit.

*Line:* Use a double taper fly line in a size that matches your rod. Many casters like to use the brightly colored orange fly lines, especially on cloudy days for visibility.

# "Dry Fly" tackle at a glance.

**Fly Rod:** 8½ to 9 ft. for 7 or 8 wt line.

**Fly:** Simple, hackled dry fly. No. 10 hook. Yellow or white.

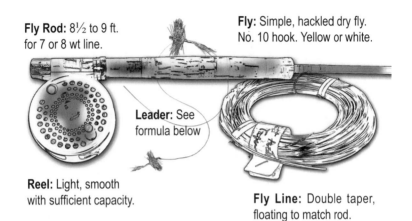

**Leader:** See formula below

**Reel:** Light, smooth with sufficient capacity.

**Fly Line:** Double taper, floating to match rod.

## L E A D E R S

| | | |
|---|---|---|
| 24 inches | 0.024" | *Formula Rajeff* |
| 18 inches | 0.021" | |
| 15 inches | 0.018" | |
| 12 inches | 0.014" | |
| 6 inches | 0.011" | **Total length:** |
| 15-18 inches | 0.009" | 7'6" - 7'9" |

| | | |
|---|---|---|
| 35 inches | 0.022" | *Formula Napoli* |
| 17 inches | 0.018" | |
| 7.5 inches | 0.016" | |
| 3.5 inches | 0.015" | |
| 3 inches | 0.014" | **Total length:** |
| 20 inches | 0.009" | 7'2" (for # 7 line) |

*Reel:* Any light reel that has sufficient capacity to hold the line comfortably will do.

*Leader:* Many expert casters claim that leader construction is as important as the rod and line. The leader formulas provided in this book were created by some of our best casters. Try them to start, but after you've gained experience, you may want to adjust them to fit your casting stroke and style.

*The Fly:* See specs in the ACA Dry Fly Rules (page 116). You can tie your own ( page 209) or purchase official tournament flies from the ACA. Many casters select yellow or white flies depending on visibility.

**THE EVENT:** There are two rounds, of five targets each, for a total of 10 targets. You start with a perfect score of 100. You are charged one demerit for each foot or fraction (max five demerits) that the fly lands away from the target. All demerits are subtracted from a perfect score of 100 for your final score. There are other demerits that we'll discuss later, but let me walk you through this event. We'll assume that you've rigged your tackle with the leader and practice fly.

1. Hold the practice fly in your noncasting hand with no more than the leader plus two feet of line extending beyond rod tip. Start false casting so that the line, leader and fly are moving in the air, back and forth without intentionally striking the surface in front of you.

While false casting, strip some fly line from your reel and let it pass through the rod guides (on the forward cast), until you think you have enough line to reach the closest target (A). If you feel that you have too much out, strip in some line while false casting (by pulling line through your index or middle finger of your casting hand with the other hand). After adjustments are made, and you feel you have enough line out, make the presentation cast and allow the fly to settle on the target.

**P-E-R-F-E-C-T!** *Congratulations!* Well done.

Okay! What if you missed the target? Don't despair; it's a

learning process. Let's continue.

2. Lift the fly off the ground (or water) and begin to false cast toward the second target. Adjust your line by stripping out line from the reel and letting it feed through the guides. If you let out too much line, strip some in. When you think you have the right amount of line out to reach the target, make your forward (presentation) cast. Keep track of your demerits (and Perfects!).

3. Proceed to Targets C, D and E. That's the first round.

4. To start the second round —the line is still extended to Target E— lift the line off the surface and continue to false cast while at the same time strip in line to shorten your cast to return to the closest target (A). This is not easy at first but with practice, it becomes automatic. Make your presentation cast to Target A.

5. Proceed to targets B, C, D and E.

That's it. In other words, you cast two rounds of five targets for a total of ten. Subtract your demerits from 100. Remember, for every foot, or fraction thereof, you have one demerit. If the fly lands 13 inches from the target, that's two demerits.

There are other demerits that eventually you must consider. The "tick" is the most important one and very frustrating especially if you have a good game going. You will remember that a tick is when your fly strikes the surface (water or ground) in front of you while you are false casting. In the dry fly event you are charged with three demerits for each tick. Sounds a bit harsh, right? Here's why: If you're false casting to a wary species, and your fly strikes the water in front of it, that fish may scoot for safety, or, at the minimum, become very suspicious of the next "meal" that floats by. Again, these tournament rules are designed to take you to another higher step in fishing skill. You will become a better angler, and if you want to cast in a tournament, you need to practice and compete within a set of rules. Imagine playing golf without demerits.

**YOUR SCORE:** Keep track of your scores in a little notebook and, if you continue to practice, you will notice a vast improvement after several weeks. There are other demerits and rules, and after you get the hang of this event you might want to study the ACA rules (page 116). You can score yourself, but it is best to practice with a friend or friends who can stand near the targets and judge more accurately.

What's a good score for fly fishers? Here's my arbitrary rating:

> **UNDER 55:** You need to learn or review fly-casting basics. Perhaps you haven't been fly casting for a long time. Go back to Section One and start with Level One. Brush up on your casting stroke and mechanics and try again.
>
> **55 to 65:** A good start! You'll notice improvement very quickly as you continue to practice.
>
> **66 to 75:** You have the basics. Practice, practice, practice.
>
> **76 to 85:** You're casting very well! Good mechanics. Good eye-and-hand coordination.
>
> **86 to 95:** I bet you're the best caster in your fishing group and catch a lot of fish. Continue to practice so that you can move up to the "super elite" class.
>
> **96 to 100** *(Super Elite Class)*: You should enter the ACA National Casting Tournament! You're among the top 1 percent of fly casters in the world!

**HOW DOES THIS DRY FLY EVENT HELP OUR FISH-ING?** Accuracy is the most important ingredient to successful fly fishing. Wouldn't it be great if you could place that fly wherever you want? While accurate casting is an advantage for nearly every species, it's particularly important in most stream trout fishing; on some brown trout waters, it is essential! When you practice casting at the targets, visualize a big trout underneath it. It helps to play mind games.

But there are other lessons to be learned from this event. The ability to strip line in and out while adjusting distances is very important. Most inexperienced casters lengthen their line by casting on the water: they make a cast, lift up the line, and make another cast on the water, and they repeat this until they reach the target. Forget it! Most wary species are long gone, especially if you "rip" the line from the surface instead of lifting it quietly with each "measuring" cast.

You will also learn to judge the distances as the fly swirls back and forth during false casting. This is vital when you are lengthening your line via false casting in order to reach a feeding trout.

You will discover that the best way of stripping in line is to pull it under the index or middle finger of your casting hand, and the best way letting line out is by controlling the amount with your left hand (if you are right handed). It takes practice before it becomes automatic.

You will learn to direct a fly accurately but at the same time have it land softly. In tournament competition, if your fly sinks on a presentation cast you receive three demerits and you're not allowed to put a floatant on the fly. Why? To get casters to land a dry fly softly. *Tip:* Some experienced tournament fly casters put more power on the final forward cast but mentally aim it about a couple of feet above the target. This cushions the cast and allows the fly to land softly.

**HOW TO MAKE THIS EVENT MORE FUN:** Keep track of your scores. By practicing often you will notice improvement on a continuing basis. Use my arbitrary scoring system and ascend from one bracket to another. This will fuel your enthusiasm for more practice.

Casting a consistently high score in the Dry Fly Event demands good fly-casting skills. Simply put, you're not going to score well if: (1) you have a poor back cast; (2) your rod tip travels in several planes; (3) your loop is too wide; or, (4) any of the other gremlins your casting instructor, fly-casting book or video warned you about. Above all, don't become discouraged. No one was born a great fly caster!

Here are some suggestions for making casting more fun:

- Involve your fishing buddies in friendly, helpful competition.

- Suggest a casting tournament to your fishing club (TU, FFF, or other).

- Teach your teenage daughter, son or spouse the fundamentals of casting and hold periodic family tournaments.

**THE CHAMPS:** At least 27 participants have cast a perfect score (100) in a National. Perhaps the most amazing perfect score was delivered by Marvin Allen, a tremendous accuracy plug caster and fierce competitor. Marv had only tried fly casting a couple of times. He was talked into competing in the Dry Fly Event at a National, and someone helped him rig up a fly outfit. Amazingly, he hit all the targets! *Perfect score!*

"Well, the fly has to land somewhere. It might as well land in a target," Allen explained with a shrug as he added another trophy to his collection.

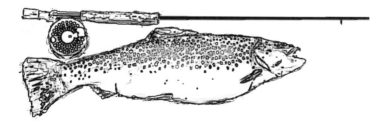

# "Trout Fly" tackle at a glance.

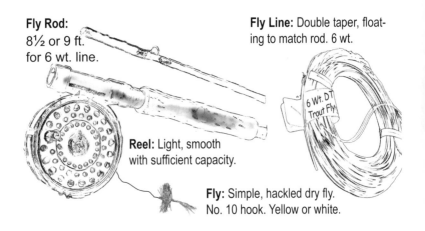

**Fly Rod:** 8½ or 9 ft. for 6 wt. line.

**Fly Line:** Double taper, floating to match rod. 6 wt.

6 Wt. DT Trout Fly

**Reel:** Light, smooth with sufficient capacity.

**Fly:** Simple, hackled dry fly. No. 10 hook. Yellow or white.

## LEADERS

| | | |
|---|---|---|
| 45 inches | 0.024" | *Formula Rajeff* |
| 18 inches | 0.021" | |
| 12 inches | 0.018" | |
| 9 inches | 0.014" | |
| 6 inches | 0.011" | **Total length:** |
| 20-22 inches | 0.008" | **9'2' - 9'4"** |

| | | |
|---|---|---|
| 18 inches | 0.032" | |
| 48 inches | 0.025" | *Formula Seroczynski* |
| 12 inches | 0.018" | |
| 6 inches | 0.015" | |
| 6 inches | 0.010" | |
| 18+inches | 0.008" | **Total length: 9'+** |

# The Trout Fly Event

A SSUMING THAT YOU'VE PRACTICED and learned
the Dry Fly Event, let's move on to one of the most exciting accuracy casting challenges: the Trout Fly Event. This is a crucial game because it stresses three very important and different casts: the Dry Fly, the Wet Fly and the Roll Cast.

**NOTE:** Unfortunately, the roll-cast round cannot be cast successfully on ground. It requires the resistance of water on the line to execute a proper roll cast. Thus, the complete event can only be cast on water.

**TARGETS:** The targets are placed exactly the same as for the Dry Fly Event, so you don't have to change them. See diagram (Page 72).

**THE TACKLE:** Within reason, you can use just about any fly-rod outfit you have for practice, provided it is not too short or too light. The tackle I suggest here is optimal for two reasons: (1) It's probably the best outfit for many freshwater fishing applications, and, (2) it will meet the requirements for casting tournaments (some of you are going to enjoy casting so much that you may want to enter local, regional or national casting tournaments).

***The Rod:*** Do you have an 8½- or 9-ft. fly rod that is calibrated for a No. 6 double-taper fly line? Perfect! Use it for this event. If you don't have one, use a fly rod that comes closest to it in terms of length and line weight. Some champion casters use a rod calibrated for a 7 or 8 wt. line, but use a 6 wt. line as specified in the ACA rules.

*The Line:* A No. 6 tapered floating line (for this event a double taper line is preferable to a forward taper).

*The Reel:* Your lightweight single-action fly reel is perfect.

*The Leader:* At least 9 ft. long (which is standard for most trout fishing) tapered to about .008" (3X) or less. Check out the leader formulas used by champion casters on page 80.

*The Fly:* You can use a fishing dry fly (No. 12), but trim it so that the wound hackle is about a ½ inch in diameter and remove the point and barb. Or, if you prefer, tie a small piece of bright yarn to the tippet. Yellow or white are the best colors. *Best Bet:* Use an ACA tournament fly.

**THE EVENT:** As mentioned, there are three different casting rounds in this event: Dry Fly, Wet Fly and the Roll Cast. A caster has 6 minutes to finish the course of three rounds or a total of 15 targets. Time begins with the first presentation cast in the Dry Fly Round.

Let's do them in that sequence:

## The Dry Fly Round

1) Hold the practice fly in the noncasting hand with no more than the leader plus two feet of line extending beyond the rod tip. Start false casting letting out line until you reach Target A (as in the previous Dry Fly Event). After visual adjustments are made, make the final forward or presentation cast and allow the fly to settle on the target. Nice going.

2) You are ready for the second target. Lift the fly off the ground or water and begin false casting again over the second target. Lengthen your line by stripping out more line from the reel and feeding it through the guides while false casting. If you let out too much line, strip some in. Make your presentation cast at Target B.

3) Proceed to the third, fourth and fifth target (C, D and E). This completes the Dry Fly Round.

If you miss the target by one foot or less you have a demerit of one. If you miss by more than one foot, the maximum demerits you receive are two. In the official tournament rules there are other demerits (such as ticks, improper strips, etc.), but right now we don't have to be concerned with them. Keep track of your score (missed targets) for the Dry Fly Round. Through sufficient practice sessions and after you've developed confidence, check on the other demerits in the ACA rules (page 118).

## The Wet Fly Round

1. Strip in the line (don't reel it in) and hold the fly in your noncasting hand with no more than two feet of fly line beyond the tip of the rod. Begin to false cast and let out line through the guides until you feel that the fly is over Target A. You can make as many false casts as you like on the first target. When you're ready, deliver your presentation cast.

2. Lift the fly line and make only one false cast in which you allow enough line to slip through the guides to reach the second target (B). After a single false cast, you must make your presentation. In other words, it's lift (back cast), forward false cast, back cast and presentation cast to the target. This shouldn't be any problem because you learned this and practiced it in the Level-To-Level series. Right? To review, you can make as many false casts as you want on the first target, but after that there is only one false cast at each target.

3. Lift the line again, make one false cast and go to the third target (C). Repeat the procedure and aim the fly to the fourth (D) and finally the fifth target (E). Remember: Only one false cast is allowed between targets. Use the same demerit system that you used for the Dry Fly Round. This is a fun round because it's fast, but at the same time it will increase your accuracy and perfect your casting loops.

Keep track of your score for the Wet Fly Round.

## The Roll Cast Round

1. After your final cast in the Wet Fly Round you retrieve the line by stripping it in until the fly is at the closest target. Don't place it on the reel. Roll cast and try to hit the first target (A). Keep roll casting until you hit it.

2. After you hit it, you go to the next closest target (B), and after you hit that, continue to the third, fourth and fifth target in the same sequence as in the two previous rounds. If you miss the target, keep roll casting until you hit it. Simple. Right?

Well, almost. I "forgot" to tell you something. You have to hit all five targets within a total of 15 roll casts. That's not easy to do, especially the two more distant targets; if there is a cross wind it becomes even more frustrating. You may need to brush up on roll casting (refer to how-to-cast videos and books by Wulff, Kreh, Krieger, Borger and others). You are charged with two demerits for each target you do not hit within the allowed 15 casts. In other words, if you hit three targets within the 15 allotted casts, you get four demerits (two demerits for each of the two targets you didn't hit).

*Tip:* The best way to lengthen the line from one target to another is to wiggle the rod tip back and forth, allowing loose line to pass through the guides. This is also a good approach in actual fishing, because if you lengthen the line by repeated roll casts, chances are the fish will be spooked or alarmed from all the swishing.

Again, you need to practice the roll cast segment on water because the ground does not create enough resistance on the line. (Some casters make "grass" leaders but I recommend roll casting on water only).

**YOUR SCORE:** Add the demerits from the Dry Fly, Wet Fly and Roll Cast rounds. Subtract the total demerits from 100 and you have your score.

It's important to keep track of your scores. As your casting skills improve, so will your scores, and this will motivate you to practice more.

Here's my arbitrary score rating for the Trout Fly Event deducting only accuracy demerits.

> **Under 70:** Something is wrong somewhere. Your math? My math? It's impossible to cast under 70, since we're not counting ticks and other nonaccuracy demerits right now. You can only get 10 demerits in each of the three rounds.

> **71 to 80:** Your casting is a little rusty, but you'll notice improvement very quickly as you continue to practice. Keep it up!

> **81 to 85:** You've got the basics down fairly well. You're doing fine.

> **86 to 90:** You're casting very well! Excellent casting mechanics. Good eye-and-hand coordination.

> **91 to 95:** Superb! What else can I say?

> **96 to 100** (*Super Elite Class*): You should enter the ACA National Casting Tournament! You're among the top one percent of fly casters in the world!

**HOW DOES THE TROUT FLY EVENT HELP YOUR FISHING?** Casting accuracy is vital in nearly all fly fishing, but especially fishing for trout and salmon.

*Dry Fly Round:* We've covered the benefits of the Dry Fly Event, so I won't repeat them here.

*The Wet Fly Round:* You're fishing a streamer, nymph, wet fly or even a dry. A trout rises to take an insect or you see that flash underneath the surface. You need to deliver the fly quickly and accurately. One false cast and deliver. In subsurface fishing you may want to cover a section systematically by "fan casting." *Lift. One false cast. Deliver.* Allow the fly to do its thing and then lift, false cast (allow some line through the guides) and deliver. Keep repeating this. Fan casting is a basic fishing approach for Atlantic salmon but can be employed with most river or stream fishing, especially when fishing wets in discolored waters.

*The Roll Cast Round:* If you fish small, brushy streams, or even big rivers where you can't make a back cast, the roll cast is imperative and essential for fishing success. You learn accuracy and how to lengthen your roll cast. Many neophytes never practice roll casting, except when absolutely necessary while fishing! Through practice, you will learn to judge the distances visually as well as develop a sense of "feel" as to how much line you need to hit that target or fish.

**HOW TO MAKE THIS MORE FUN:** Again you should keep track of your scores. If you practice often, you will notice improvement on a continuing basis. Use my arbitrary scoring system presented above and try to move from one level of skill to another. This will increase your enthusiasm for more practice.

The Trout Fly Event teaches you three important types of casting. In fact, if you learn these three casts well, your fishing results will zoom. *Guaranteed!*

As in the Dry Fly Event, encourage your friends, family, fishing club, TU or other organizations to become involved in this wholesome, rewarding and enjoyable activity.

Learning the Trout Fly Event is challenging. Practice it! Don't give up easily. Suddenly it will come to you, and your confidence in casting will result in more and bigger fish.

**THE CHAMPS:** Many have shot perfect scores at local and

regional ACA tournaments, but in the Nationals only Chris Korich, Steve Rajeff, Tim Rajeff and Zack Willson have cast 100s. Not an easy event.

*Paul Melchior has fished many of the world's finest waters. He credits tournament and practice casting for his ample successes.*

# "Bass Bug" tackle at a glance.

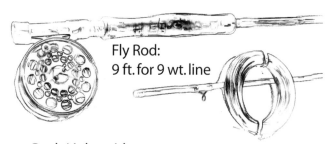

Fly Rod:
9 ft. for 9 wt. line

Reel: Light, with
sufficient capacity.

Fly Line: Weight forward
for bass bugs. 9 wt.

## L E A D E R S

| | | |
|---|---|---|
| 30 inches | 0.028" | *Formula Rajeff* |
| 18 inches | 0.024" | |
| 9 inches | 0.021" | |
| 6 inches | 0.018" | |
| 15-18 inches | 0.014" | *Total length: 6'6" - 6'9"* |

| | | |
|---|---|---|
| 43 inches | 0.030" | *Formula Napoli* |
| 13 inches | 0.028" | |
| 9 inches | 0.022" | |
| 7 inches | 0.019" | |
| 3 inches | 0.017" | |
| 12 inches | 0.014" | *Total length: 7'4"* |

# The Bass Bug Event

T HE DRY FLY AND TROUT FLY EVENTS focus on casting small flies at reasonable distances. How about a game for anglers who toss poppers, air-resistant flies or streamers for bass, pike, muskies, snook, permit or other species? The challenging Bass Bug Event is the answer for many fishing applications that require big flies.

**THE TARGETS:** . So far we've used only five targets. For this event, we need a sixth target. Use the same setup for the first five targets as in the Dry Fly Event but place the sixth target 65 to 70 feet from the caster's box (page 72). Yeah, you're right! That's a tough cast with even a tiny fly, let alone an air-resistant popper. But, with practice, we'll get it done. The Bass Bug Event is great for learning to cast the big flies far and accurately.

**THE TACKLE:** We'll use heavier gear than what we've recommended for the two previous events, because we're going to cast a bass popper, which is a lot more air resistant and heavier than a dry fly. Here are tackle recommendations for this event:

*The Rod:* A 9-ft. fly rod calibrated to take a No. 8 or a 9 fly line is ideal. If you don't have a nine footer but have an 8½-ft. fly rod, use it, although the extra length is helpful.

*The Line:* A No. 8 or 9 forward tapered **floating** line is best.

*The Reel:* Your normal single-action fly reel is fine as long as it holds the line comfortably and is not too heavy.

*The Leader:* At least 6 feet in length tapered from about .028" to about .014" or less. Best Bet: Use the recommended bass bug formulas on page 88.

*The Bug:* You can use just about any cork body bass bug, but be sure to remove the point and barb to avoid any accidents; however, it's best to use a bass bug that simulates the official ACA popper. The cork body should be at least ¾ inch in length and no less than ½ inch in diameter. The hair tail should be an inch or longer. The ideal color for visibility is yellow or white (see page 209).

**HOW TO CAST THE BASS BUG EVENT:** Start by stripping sufficient line from your reel so that it is at least ten feet beyond the far target which is about 65 to 70 feet away. Now strip in all the line (don't reel it in) so that you have no more than two feet of fly line and your leader beyond the rod tip.

# Round One

1. Hold the bass bug in your noncasting hand. Begin false casting and let sufficient line pass through the rod guides to reach the first target. After adjustments are made, and your bass bug seems to hover above the near target (A) on your false cast, make your first presentation cast by allowing the bug to settle, hopefully, right in the center of the target. You don't have to make a delicate presentation, so put some force behind the forward cast, because you want to straighten out that leader. Remember: You can make as many false casts as you like until the first presentation cast to Target A. So take your time.

2. Lift the bug off the ground or water and begin false casting again over the second target (B). Let out line through the guides as needed. If you let out too much line, strip some in. When you think the bug will land in the center of the target, make your presentation cast and drop the popper on the target. Easy, huh? Okay, here's the catch. Except for the first target, you can only make **two false casts** between the remaining

targets. In other words, you have to make a quick adjustment of the amount of line needed to reach the target.

Why only two false casts? Suppose you're fishing and you notice a marauding bass chasing some minnows just beyond your popper. If you make a lot of false casts that fish is LG (*long gone*). You have to deliver the popper or bug accurately, decisively and quickly. The same applies for tarpon, snook and just about any gamefish.

3. Proceed to the third (C), fourth (D) and fifth target (E). You'll notice that the distant targets are harder to hit.

4. After you make your cast to the fifth target (E) you've got the long one (F) that's 65-70 feet away! That's a real toughie! Unless you are a very good caster (or very lucky), that last target is a killer. And remember you can only make two false casts between targets!

The first thing you learn is that it is impossible to reach the distant target without being able to execute the double haul. It's frustrating. It's challenging. But what a sense of accomplishment when you learn to do it and hit that far target!

That takes care of the Round One. (If you think that round was challenging, wait until the next one). Here we go:

## Round Two

1. Strip in line (don't reel it in) until you have only about two feet of line plus the leader beyond the rod tip and the hookless bass bug is in your non-casting hand.

2. You'll do the same thing as in Round One. Make as many false casts as you'd like to the close target before making your presentation cast, which is scored. You're going to cast to the next five targets in the same sequence as in Round One, but on this round you will only make *one false cast between the targets*. I know it's tough, but these events are designed to improve your casting by challenging your skills to the max.

That sixth target—where you go from 45-50 feet to 65-70 feet with one false cast—is a button buster. To do this, you must execute a fairly smooth double haul.

I said at the beginning that this event is difficult and demanding; however, the purpose of these "games" is to make you the very best caster you can possibly be. If you practice these casting disciplines you will see a constant improvement and the rewards are twofold: You will enjoy the effortless casting while fishing, and your angling success will definitely improve. You'll feel an absolute "high" when you deliver that popper right next to that stump 70 feet away!

*Caution:* You have to be careful in lifting up the line from Target E (45-50 ft.) to cast to Target F (65-70 ft.) so that you don't damage the rod. Yes, it requires some *oomph* but you have to learn to peel the line from the surface and at the same time accelerate the back cast with a haul.

If you are having problems reaching the distant targets, move them in five to ten feet and adjust the others accordingly. Then, as you gain casting efficiency and confidence move them out. Some fly-casting outfits were not built to cast a bass bug 50 to 70 feet. Don't try to do this event with your No. 5 or 6 trout fishing outfit!

**SCORING:** Run through this event a few times, without scoring. After you get the hang of it, you can score your results as follows: You start with 100 points. There is one demerit for each foot (or fraction thereof) that the bug misses the target. There is a maximum of two demerits for the first five targets. Yes, the people who designed these rules have some compassion after all!

Well, not quite, because on the last target (F), the one that is w-a-y out there, they increased the maximum demerits to five in both rounds. Obviously, that last target is extremely important. There are other demerits: Each tick gives you one demerit, and if you make more false casts than the allotted number (two false casts in first round and one false cast in second round), you're charged with one demerit for each additional false cast (page 121).

**YOUR SCORE:** As we have mentioned ad nauseam, it's important to keep track of your scores, so that you can see your improvement with casting practice.

Here's my arbitrary rating for the Bass Bug Event. (We'll not count ticks or demerits for additional false casts here.)

> **Under 70:** Impossible. If you miss every target by the max, your score would be 70, since we're not counting ticks and additional false casts here.

> **71 to 75:** Hey, this is a tough event. You'll get the hang of it.

> **76 to 83:** You've got the basics and all you need to do is practice.

> **84 to 90:** You're casting very well! Good eye-and-hand coordination. Terrific!

> **91 to 95**: Superb! *You are an excellent caster.*

> **96 to 100 (Super-Elite Class)**: If you are making the right number of false casts and not ticking, you are ACA National Casting Tournament Championship caliber! You're among the top 1 percent of fly casters in the world! Very few of the top casting instructors are going to score in this bracket!

**HOW DOES THE BASS BUG EVENT HELP YOUR FISHING?** If you fish with big flies (bass bugs, poppers, large streamers, etc.), this event will help you immensely. *Important:* One of the lessons you will learn is that, when casting air-resistant poppers or large weighted flies, you will have to wait a little longer on your back cast than you normally would if you were casting small trout flies. This is crucial!

Being able to pick up a lot of line and deliver a long accurate cast is certainly very helpful in just about every saltwater fly-fishing application. Bonefishing. Tarpon. Snook. Permit.

Redfish. The same applies to sight fishing in freshwater: Big northern pike or muskies cruising the shallows. Steelhead. Salmon. Bass. Many species. We've all had the experience that no matter how much power we were able to put into the cast, we were six to ten feet short of a feeding fish. If our casting limit is, say, 50 feet, the fish are 60 feet away. Frustrating, right? We eventually find out that **timing is more important than "muscle."**

You'll quickly learn the importance of a good back cast, loading a rod, double haul, how to pick up a longer line, how to cast an air-resistant large fly or popper with accuracy and many other techniques that are so necessary in many fishing presentations.

**THE CHAMPS:** After you try this event a few times, you probably wonder what scores win in the ACA National Tournament. Usually, 96 and above, and, yes, there have been some perfect scores. Amazingly, when Luke Brugnara was an intermediate caster (age 13 -16), he cast a perfect score! Tim Rajeff, Chris Korich and Steve Rajeff have also cast 100s.

Alice Gillibert cast a perfect 100 in the Bass Bug Event in a registered ACA tournament (not in a National).

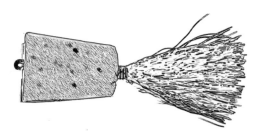

# The Angler's Fly Distance Event

OKAY, YOU'VE PRACTICED accuracy casting to targets, and hopefully had a chance to make some accurate casts to fish, too. Great! Now we're going to advance to the distance events.

While accurate casting is the more important factor in fishing success, we've all experienced times when we needed to cast an extra ten feet or more to reach a feeding trout, a tailing bonefish or a bass tearing up a school of fleeing minnows. Putting extra muscle into the cast isn't going to do it if the timing is missing.

Many anglers can cast 45 to 50 feet without employing the single- or double-haul casting technique. If you want to make longer casts or if you want to make 50- to 70-foot casts with less effort and more grace, you must learn to double haul.

You may want to take an advance casting course if one's available near you—one that heavily concentrates on the double haul and is taught by an experienced double-haul instructor—or you may want to study books and videos by Joan Wulff, Mel Krieger, Lefty Kreh, Jason Borger and others. As I've explained previously, this is **not** a how-to-cast book; instead, its mission is to get you to practice certain events or games so that you will become the best caster you can possibly be.

The Angler's Fly Distance Event will help you add considerable distance to your normal cast.

# Angler's Distance at a glance.

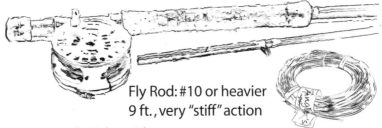

Fly Rod: #10 or heavier
9 ft., very "stiff" action

Reel: Light, with
sufficient capacity.

Fly Line: 28 to 31 ft. head.
310 grains or less. (#10).
Shooting line: No less than
0.015 in. mono.

### LEADERS

| 48 inches | 0.022" | *Formula Rajeff* |
| 24 inches | 0.018" | |
| 12 inches | 0.016" | |
| 24-60 inches | 0.014" | |

*Total length: 9 to 12 ft.*

| 48 inches | 0.022" | *Formula Korich* |
| 24 (36) inches | 0.018" | |
| 12 (24) inches | 0.016" | |
| 24-30 (30-36) inches | 0.014" | |

*Total length: 9 to 12 ft.*

NOTE: The shorter leaders are used in calm weather;
the longer leaders are for favorable windy conditions.

**THE TACKLE:** If you're fishing a brushy stream or a small river, you're not going to need very long casts and a 3 to 5 weight fly rod is fine for small rivers. But if you are going to fish big rivers, bonefish or tarpon flats, big pike and muskies and similar applications where a longer-than-normal cast is usually required, you will be using a heavier rod. This event is designed for heavier tackle and longer casts.

Here are some tackle suggestions that closely conform to the American Casting Association (ACA) tournament rules. I know that some of you will enjoy these events to a point that you may eventually compete in tournaments. Bear in mind, you can use just about any equipment except the most delicate, light fly rod for this event, but I suggest you try to come close to the following gear.

*The Rod:* A 9-ft. graphite calibrated for a No. 10 shooting head is ideal.

*The Reel:* A light fly reel that has sufficient capacity.

*The Line:* This gets a little tricky. You want a shooting head (No. 10) between 28 and 31 feet in length that weighs no more than 310 grains.

*The Running Line:* Use a monofilament that's .015" in diameter or thicker.

*The Leader:* Nine to 12 ft. leader tied from hard or stiff mono that tapers from .022" to about .014." Refer to the recommended leader formulas on page 96.

*The Fly:* Attach a brightly colored No. 10 or 12 fly (but be sure to remove the barb and point at the bend of the hook for practice) or simply tie on a small piece of yarn. In ACA tournaments, you must use a standard distance fly.

**WHERE TO PRACTICE:** This event is best practiced on land. It's easier to pick up the line off the grass and you can easily measure your casts. Today, all ACA distance-casting tournaments are held on land.

**TARGETS:** None. This is a distance event. You need a long tape (150-ft. or longer) or you can make your own measuring device. See page 19.

Before you begin to practice your distance for measurement, stretch out the measuring line or tape and place some markers at each increment (75, 100, 125 or more feet). A marker can be just about anything that's highly visible: brightly colored cloth, traffic cone or a hat.

You need one more thing: A simple scorecard (page 212). Record your longest casts every time you practice so that you can gauge your day-to-day improvement. Before casting distance, limber up for a few minutes with some stretching exercises and a few short and easy casts. Do not try to cast distance without a short warm-up period and some shorter casts.

**HOW TO CAST THE ANGLER'S FLY DISTANCE EVENT:** Nothing complicated here. Step right up, ladies and gentlemen, and let 'er rip!!!

Okay, okay. So you got the line tangled around your neck, and you tried to put too much *oomph* into your cast. Let's back off a bit. Let's take it *e-a-s-y.*

First, you need to know the double haul. You must understand the principle of the double haul in order to attain distance. And you must practice it. You can practice the double-haul casting motion even without a rod or reel and expert casters often recommend it. Kids practice "air guitar," right?

(*Tip:* Don't practice "air casting" in a supermarket, or during intermission at a concert, or while listening to a less-than-inspiring sermon. Not everyone understands the double-haul motion or what it's for. If you *insist* on practicing the motion in public, take along the butt section of an old fly rod. People will then know that you're an angler and pay no further attention to you.)

Back to casting. You will note that the shooting head must be beyond the rod tip (known as "overhang") during your false casts, and this takes a little experimentation. If you have about three feet of line beyond the rod tip during your extended left hand pull on the double haul, that's a good starting point. You may have to let out a little line or take some in. This adjustment of overhang is very critical and competent casters may disagree as to the exact amount of overhang, because much depends on casting style, stroke, double-haul pull, tackle and other variables. The amount of overhang is crucial because it determines the size and shape of the loop. You need to experiment on overhang.

You will find that the narrow loop, timing, trajectory, stroke and equipment determine the distances, but wind and weather conditions are also very important. Even a barely perceivable breeze, humidity and ground elevation can alter your distance positively or negatively.

Unless you are a very experienced caster, take your time and don't try to throw the cast into the next zip code. Concentrate on timing, throwing a narrow loop and not hitting yourself on the cast. T-i-m-i-n-g in coordinating the double haul and applied casting power is the key to long distance success. Remember: The line will follow the path of the rod tip.

I don't know why it is, my friends, but it seems that an angler may spend hours developing a golf swing or putting, working on an explosive tennis serve, or shooting clay targets. For some incomprehensible reason, many feel that casting shouldn't require much practice and that casting skill should almost be a birthright! Not so.

Casting requires as much practice as learning to hit a baseball, playing the piano or any of thousands of activities. The more you practice *intelligently,* the better you become. Oh, you'll have your good days, and the bad ones, too, but practice develops consistency.

So you practice and practice, and maybe you become a little discouraged at times, but keep at it and it will come to you. One day, soon, you're going to get off that cast that just sails and sails, and goes so far that it will give you such a *high*, that you will always remember that cast. That is, until you make an even better, longer cast.

Keep track of your scores and you'll notice the improvement, which will fuel your desire to practice more. After you warm up, don't distance cast for more than five minutes, because it is very tiring on certain muscles and you will slip into bad casting habits.

**Suggested schedule:** Five minutes of vigorous distance casting, relax for ten, then another five minutes of practice, then go home and drink a glass or two of water, tie flies or whatever. Later on, you can increase the number of casting sessions to about eight minutes and do three or four sets before relaxing.

What is great about this casting game is that you can practice it just about anywhere and at any age (unless you are physically challenged). There are guys in their upper 70s who can cast further than *some* of the experts who are half their age and twice as strong. Why is that? Because they understand the principles of the casting stroke, applied power, the importance of controlled loops and because they continue to practice.

**WHAT ABOUT DISTANCES?** Again, this is subjective, but here are some benchmarks:

> **60-70 feet or less:** Good going. It's a start.
>
> **70 to 90 feet:** Consider yourself a fairly good caster (you are throwing a heavy shooting head, which, for some people, is harder to cast than a lighter outfit with a standard fly line).
>
> **90 to 110 feet:** You've learned the double haul well and with more practice can develop into a very good distance caster.
>
> **110 to 125 feet:** Superb. With a few tips from an experienced distance fly caster you could move up into the next bracket.

**125 or 140 feet:** See what I mean about getting a *high* when you uncork a long cast! Great, isn't it? **You bet!**

**140 or more feet:** Okay, okay you're a tournament caster and you're reading these pages out of curiosity, right? You can't fool me. If you aren't a tournament caster, you're one heckuva good caster and definitely ACA National Casting Championship material!

## HOW DOES THIS EVENT RELATE TO FISHING?

Distance casting and the double haul are essential whenever a longer-than-normal cast is necessary, such as, when fishing for steelhead, salmon, bonefish and tarpon. Do you need casts of over 100 feet? Of course not! Well, almost never. But what we learn in this event is to how make long casts. It teaches us how to apply line speed, develop the double haul and timing so necessary to deliver bulkier fly patterns, bass bugs and other air-resistant lures to unusually long distances.

**THE CHAMPS:** Steve Rajeff (in my opinion, the world's best all-round caster *ever)*, cast 190 feet at a National tournament and so did Rene Gillibert. Bill Clements, a senior caster (over 60 years old) cast 166 feet (2005). Alice Gillibert threw a fly 150 feet at the 2004 National to set the women's record. George Revel, intermediate caster (13 through 16), cast 154 feet (2005 National).

The distances are determined **where the fly lands** and not how much line goes through the guides. Often a caster can get 150 feet of line (shooting head and running line) beyond the rod tip, but the end of the fly line and the long leader do not straighten out and may fall back 20 feet or more. Result? A 130-foot cast. Or less.

Thus Alice Gillibert's cast of 150 feet—that's half of a football field—is incredible. And Steve Rajeff's and Rene Gillibert's 190-ft. casts defy the laws of gravity!

# The One-Hand Fly Distance Event

IN THE PREVIOUS CHAPTER we featured the Angler's Fly Distance Event, which some West Coasters refer to as the "Steelhead Distance Event" because the equipment is similar to what's used in steelhead fishing on the big rivers. The Angler's Fly Distance has wide salt and freshwater applications. It's a great practice event for just about any type of fishing that requires longer-than-normal casting distance. The One-Hand Fly Distance Event is really an extension of the Angler's Fly Distance except that much heavier tackle is used. In these events, only one hand is on the rod, but, of course, the other hand is just as important in that it helps execute the double haul.

The One-Hand Fly Distance is a "controversial" event. Its detractors claim that it requires tremendous strength and stamina and has only a vague connection to fishing because of the specialized equipment. Its disciples counter that Rene Gillibert, who is not a big guy, has cast a fly more than 200 feet in this event. Rene is strong for his size, but relies on split-second timing and incredible coordination. Think of it: That's two-thirds of a football field! The disciples also can claim that Ed Lanser and Zack Willson, in their 70s, who now compete in the Senior's Division (competitors must be over 60 years old), have cast 180 feet in Nationals. Furthermore, Joan Wulff, who is about 5'5" tall, threw a fly 161 feet in a registered tournament years ago. Again timing and coordination are obviously more important than brute strength.

The big difference between the Angler's Fly Distance and the

# One-Hand Distance at a glance.

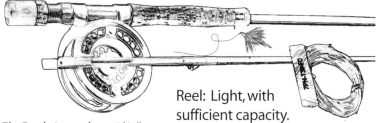

Fly Rod: Less than 9'9."
Must be very stiff (#14 +)

Reel: Light, with
sufficient capacity.

Fly Line: Head must be 49'3" or longer and weigh no
more than 650 grains.  Shooting Line: Unrestricted.
(Try 8- or 10- lb. mono).  Holding Line: Use about 20 ft. of
25-lb. mono between head and shooting line (to
prevent breakage).

## LEADERS

| | |
|---|---|
| 36-48 inches | 0.022" |
| 24-36 inches | 0.018" |
| 12-24 inches | 0.016" |
| 24-36 inches | 0.014 |

*Formula Rajeff*

**Total length: 8 to 12 ft.**

| | |
|---|---|
| 36 (48) inches | 0.025" |
| 18 (24) inches | 0.022" |
| 6 (12) inches | 0.018" |
| 24 inches | 0.017" |

*Formula Korich*

**Total length: 7 (9) ft.**

NOTE: The shorter leaders are used in calm weather;
the longer leaders are for favorable windy conditions.

One-Hand Event is that the latter employs a heavier, longer line, which requires a much stronger fly rod than you're going to find in fly shops. The American Casting Association (ACA) states that the shooting head "shall not be less than 49 feet, 3 inches in length." Another rule is that the shooting head can't weigh more than 650 grains.

Now, false casting a high-density 50-foot shooting head plus leader is not easy. You'll huff and puff and use all your stamina to get that blasted line moving to and fro. You also need to increase the line speed and execute a perfect double haul on that final cast. And if it's done right? *Zoom!* That line will sail and sail.

Why bother presenting the controversial One-Hand Fly Distance Event here? Several reasons: (1) it teaches us important timing lessons that can reflect positively on certain fly-fishing applications; (2) once you get the hang of it, it's fun; (3) it's a tremendous exercise that burns up calories and, if practiced regularly, will keep you fit (I find that ten minutes of this event is more tiring than an hour of moderate exercise at the health club); and, (4) because it's my favorite event (hey, as author, I get some perks, you know).

The One-Hand Fly Distance Event is frustrating, but challenging. It's exhausting, but soothing. Dumb, in one way, but compelling in another. Degrading (such as when oodles of line drapes around your ears on a cast), and ego inflating when you unleash a cast of more than 150 feet. There will be times when you'll seriously consider selling this specialized equipment in a garage sale and going back to your 4-weight rod forever; however, on other days, when you succeed, you'll wonder, why isn't this wonderful event in the Olympics?

What the One-Hand Distance Fly Event teaches you is the importance of a tight loop, flawless casting stroke, timing and the precise execution of the double haul. By learning this on a heavy outfit, where every motion and action is exaggerated, you'll be able to handle any "normal" fly rod with ease.

You've observed that home-run hitters swing a heavy iron bar or two bats together prior to stepping up to the plate, right? Same principle.

**THE EVENT:** Please refer to *The Target and Distance Markers* (page 18) for acquiring or making a simple measuring tape. The ACA rules are basically simple: You cast this event on grass and make as many casts as you want to within a five-minute period and the two longest casts are marked. In competition, the person who makes the longest cast is declared the winner. If there is a tie, the second longest cast determines the winner.

It helps if you can practice with an interested friend, because you can take turns casting and measuring casts and observing each other's casting technique and making suggestions. You help each other.

"What if I can't find anyone crazy enough to practice this event?" No problem. You can do it by yourself. You place markers at various intervals (e.g., 100, 125 and 150 feet) so that you can more easily gauge the distances and record your best casts in your scorecard. As you continue to practice, you will observe periodic progress. Try to remember what you did after each cast. When you make a longer-than-normal distance cast, duplicate it. How much overhang did you allow? Where did you stop on your back cast? When did you begin your haul on the final forward cast? Things like that.

**Tip:** Don't even consider trying to cast this event unless you have mastered the double haul. It's essential.

**Another Tip:** Because of the longer shooting head in this event, it's important to turn your head around to observe your back cast. A smooth well-executed back cast is equally if not more important than your forward cast. Phenom caster Steve Rajeff does this all the time. He wants to know exactly what his back cast is doing and is constantly adjusting his stroke, overhang and timing based on what he sees and the current weather conditions.

**Another Tip:** You know that video camera you use mostly for recording family barbecues and weddings? Set it up on a tripod and record your casting. Then play the video on your TV and analyze your casting in slow motion and normal modes. Even if you have only a moderate knowledge of fly casting, you will notice your flaws and correct them during the next casting session (see page 130 for details).

**And Still Another Tip:** You absolutely don't want to practice this event for more than five minutes at a time because you will tire and develop bad casting habits.

**THE TACKLE:** I'm going to give you a simplified version of the ACA tackle requirements for this event and then some suggestions.

*The Fly Rod:* Not to exceed 9 feet, 9 inches. Who'd want a longer one? Who could handle it? (Okay, maybe Shaq O'Neal. Maybe.)

*The Reel:* Unrestricted (but use a lightweight reel).

*The Shooting Head:* Not less than 49 feet, three inches (49'3") in length, and may not weigh more than 650 grains (again, who could handle a heavier line). You can obtain shooting heads designed for this event from the American Casting Association. Obtain either the 38-gram line if you are a strong caster or the lighter 36-gram line.

*The Holding Line:* Use about 20 feet of 20-pound mono. Tie one end of the holding line to the head and the other end to the running line. Two purposes: It helps prevent breakage of the light running line and it's easier to hold.

*The Running Line:* Unrestricted (nearly all competitors use monofilament). After you get the hang of this event, use the lightest possible mono you can handle (without breaking off).

*The Leader:* Single strand, not shorter than six feet or longer than 12 feet. Use the longer leader when you have a favoring breeze (see page 103).

*The Fly:* The hackle cannot be smaller than 5/8 inch in diam-

eter. Official flies are used for registered ACA tournaments. (If you are using a fishing fly, please, please remove the point and barb when practicing…or tie on a small piece of yarn. And wear glasses whenever you are casting for safety reasons).

**MORE ON TACKLE:** The problem is that, to cast this event competitively, you will need a very powerful fly rod (No. 14 or heavier) because of the length and weight of the head. Actually, if it weren't for the minimum shooting head length, this line would be manageable on lighter rods. Since the AFTMA standard line rating system is based on the weight (in grains) for the **first 30 feet**, it would be about a No. 12; however, because of the minimum length (almost 50 feet), it's equivalent to a No. 17 line. See why you need stamina to cast this event?

For most of us, this gear is not practical or readily available. We're going to assume that you are **not** going to compete in the ACA One-Hand Fly Distance Championship. At least, not right now. However, you'd like to learn this event and have some fun and perhaps *wow* your fishing friends when you unleash some very long casts at the next fly-fishing club picnic.

First of all, the rules state that the line **cannot be more than** 650 grains for the 50-foot length. It can be lighter. I think nearly all the top casters use somewhat lighter lines and these guys are terrific casters. You might have to experiment a little, because it depends on what type of heavy fly rods you have. If you have a No. 12- or 13-weight fly rod and some high density fly lines that you can cut up and splice, you can eventually put together an outfit that is usable for this event. Although you don't have to follow ACA's rules—unless you're competing in its tournaments—you want to come as close as possible to the length of the shooting head. Try a 40-ft. shooting head as a starter and use a .015 in. Amnesia mono (or similar) for a running line to start. Then as you become reasonably comfortable, use a longer head and a lighter shooting line.

I like the One-Hand Fly Distance Event for reasons I've mentioned above, despite the fact that one must obtain special equipment to compete in the ACA sanctioned tournaments. (Scientific Anglers makes a number of gray fly lines strictly for the tournament casters, and several rod makers offer heavy sticks for this event. AirFlo also makes a fly line for this event. It's orange and easier to see. They are obtainable through the ACA).

In my opinion, the line length (30 feet) of the Angler's Distance Fly is too short, and the One-Hand Distance fly line (almost 50 feet) is too long. A 38- to 40-ft. shooting head would be ideal as an official ACA event because: 1) it's the easiest length head to handle for distance casting; 2) a number of manufacturers make these shooting heads and are readily available; and, 3) there are many fly rod models capable of handling this length line.

**WHAT ABOUT DISTANCES:** Normally in these lessons I like to provide benchmarks, but because this event is heavily based on specialized equipment, not readily available, it's difficult. But assuming that you put together the right outfit based on ACA rules, and that you've mastered the double haul, here are some numbers:

**100 to 125 feet:** While this distance is not going to win

ACA tournaments, it indicates that you understand the basics and with some practice you will quickly ascend to the next level.

**126 to 145 feet:** You're an excellent distance caster. Keep it up! You're on your way!

**146 to 165 feet:** Wonderful! Feel proud! You have climbed a peak that very few anglers have reached. You're a very gifted distance caster.

**Over 165 feet:** *Elite class!* Surely you've done lots of tournament casting. Less than 40 anglers/casters in North America can cast this far under normal weather conditions.

**THE LONGEST CAST:** Steve Rajeff cast 248 feet at the World Casting Championship in Pretoria, South Africa. His longest cast at an ACA National was 236 feet!

# Two-Hand Distance at a glance.

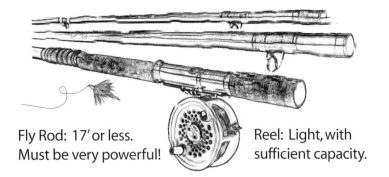

Fly Rod: 17' or less. Must be very powerful!

Reel: Light, with sufficient capacity.

Fly Line: Head must be 49'3" or longer and weigh no more than 1855 grains. Shooting Line: Unrestricted. (Try 10- or 12- lb. mono). Holding Line: Use about 30 ft. of 50-lb. mono between head and shooting line (to prevent breakage and slippage).

## LEADERS

| | |
|---|---|
| 60 inches | 0.028" |
| 36-48 inches | 0.024" |
| 36 inches | 0.022" |
| 36-60 inches | 0.018" |

### *Formula Rajeff*

**Total length: 14 to 17 ft.**

| | |
|---|---|
| 60 inches | 0.033" |
| 36 (48) inches | 0.028" |
| 24 (36) inches | 0.025" |
| 12 (24) inches | 0.022" |
| 24 (36) inches | 0.018" |

### *Formula Korich*

**Total length: 13 (17) ft.**

NOTE: The shorter leaders are used in calm weather; the longer leaders are for favorable windy conditions.

# The Two-Hand
# Fly Distance Event

IF SOME CRITICS OF TOURNAMENT CASTING
consider the One-Hand Fly Distance Event ridiculous, they
would certainly shake their heads if they witnessed the Two-
Hand Fly Distance Event. They would, however, agree that it
requires considerable athleticism and perfect timing to throw
a fly 290 feet, which is what Steve Rajeff did at an ACA
National tournament.

Yes, 290 feet! Almost an entire football field.

"Why on earth would a human being want to cast a fly that
far in fishing?" many observers have asked. They are right.
The Two-Hand Fly Distance only faintly mirrors fishing
situations.

Then why do casters do it? Because it's a challenge. For the
same reason that athletes train and train to throw a javelin
some incredible distance, or whirl and twirl and huff and
puff, to toss a 16-pound shot put! Why do some of us run
an exhausting marathon? Why do some people drive a car
around a track hundreds of times, at incredible speeds, and
end up just about where they started? We are practical in
many ways, but we also like challenges, and the Two-Hand
Distance Event is exactly that: a tremendous challenge.

I'm not a fan of the Two-Hand Fly Distance Event but I
understand its appeal for those who seek immense challenges
with a "fly rod." I've tried it in tournaments. I cast it in
the 2002 National and threw a fly 162 feet. That's half of a
football field. Pretty good, right? Terrible! I ended up second

from the bottom. And that was in the Senior's (60 years or older) classification.

While the equipment is heavy (the rod is 17 feet long!) and the event is very enervating, it is, at the same time a very graceful athletic accomplishment. In this event, there is no double haul, and both hands are on the rod.

I enjoy watching it. I enjoy seeing Steve Rajeff, Chris Korich, Henry Mittel and the other young pups cast the long fly, but I particularly like to watch casters such as Dick Fujita, who is 79 year old, not big, and has outlasted several pacemakers. Fujita lifts that heavy "fly rod," masterfully waves the long, high density line a couple of times, and then with perfect timing sends the fly past 200 feet.

Canadian Gord Deval, 76, who survived several near death experiences, loves the Two-Hand Event, and casts well over 200 feet. Ed Lanser, another senior caster with serious health concerns, set the record for seniors with an explosive cast of 266 feet. My goodness, how do these people do it? I ask.

It's coordination, they explain, knowing when and how to apply the final power stroke, pulling the bottom of the rod with one hand, while pushing with another, rigging the right leader, controlling the line loops. Many things.

To really appreciate these tremendous casts, one needs only to pick up a Two-Hand outfit. Unless you've spent a lifetime pushing weights, you'll be shocked at the weight of the rod. Most of the distance casters use 17 ft. rods (the longest allowed in ACA and international competition), with a 1+ in. diameter at the butt. But you really can't appreciate the tremendous physical demands of this event unless you rig the outfit, attach a leader and fly and try to cast it.

The problem is compounded because the shooting head has to be a minimum of 49 ft. 3 in. (15 meters). It must not weigh more than 1800 grains, and I believe all casters use a high-density line (thin diameter, but heavy). When you add the

required leader
(6 to 17 feet),
plus the overhang,
you've got quite
a load. You need
to "aerialize" the
line and to develop
speed. You must then
execute a powerful
thrust on the forward
cast, stopping the rod tip
high and abruptly in such
a way that the line zooms
skyward, up and fast. And if
you do everything just right,
*wow*, that line soars. I can't
personally describe that rush,
because this is a casting "high"
I've not experienced. But I observe
the casters who throw those incredible towering 240-ft.-plus
casts and their sense of accomplishment easily transmits to an
appreciative audience.

This game is similar to the Single-Hand Fly Distance Event,
except that the good casters need a lot more real estate
because of their longer casts.

In the Single-Hand Event, a caster has five minutes to make
his longest casts, but in the Two-Hand Event he is allowed
seven minutes, presumably because it requires more time to
strip in the line from the longer casts usually achieved in the
Two-Hand game. In both of these events, a ghillie is allowed
on an optional basis. The ghillie can strip in the line and help
the caster prepare for the next cast.

Most casters do not use ghillies in the Single Hand, but many
do in the Two-Hand Event because just holding that 17-ft. rod
is work enough.

The use of the ghillie (guide) stems back through the centuries when the English anglers hired a ghillie to tend to their tackle while they fished for salmon.

Much of the Two-Hand Event is based on the English salmon tradition, and in fact it was once called Salmon Fly Distance.

My personal opinion is that this event could become popular with anglers if the tackle were scaled down. Instead of 17-ft. rods, why not make the maximum length 15 feet? Why not limit the lines to a 12-weight? Recently the two-hand fly rod has gained tremendous popularity in North America.

The distance boys could make their awesome casts, and while the scores would not be as impressive, this event could attract many more anglers to the casting game.

# American Casting Association
## RULES AND REGULATIONS
### FOR ACCURACY AND DISTANCE FLY EVENTS

The American Casting Association (ACA) was founded in 1906 and is composed of clubs and individual members in the United States and Canada. The ACA is the control organization for the sport of competitive tournament casting. The main objective of the ACA is to educate all interested individuals or groups in angling and casting as a recreational activity.

All casters competing in ACA Registered Tournaments and the Annual ACA National Tournament are required to follow these rules. This is a simpler, condensed version, giving the caster the necessary information so that he/she can better enjoy the sport of casting and become familiar with the various distance and accuracy fly events.

## DIVISIONS & CLASSES OF CASTERS

| | |
|---|---|
| **MEN:** | Men 17 years of age or older |
| **WOMEN:** | Women 17 years of age or older |
| **SENIOR MEN:** | Men 60 years or older |
| **SENIOR WOMEN:** | Women 60 years or older |
| **INTERMEDIATE:** | Boys and girls 13 thru 16 years of age |
| **JUNIORS:** | Boys and girls 9 thru 12 years of age |
| **YOUTH:** | Boys and girls under 9 years of age |
| *CLASS A:* | A caster scoring 95 points or above |
| *CLASS B:* | A caster scoring between 85 and 94 |
| *CLASS C:* | A caster scoring under 85 |

**Note:** Casters may be divided into Class A, B and C in registered ACA tournaments, but there is no class distinction in National Tournaments, only divisions.

# FLY ACCURACY EVENTS

There are three fly accuracy events: Dry Fly Accuracy, Trout Fly Accuracy and Bass Bug Accuracy.

## DRY FLY ACCURACY

### Target Course

The targets are 30-inch diameter rings and set in water. The nearest target is 20 to 25 feet from the center of the edge of the casting box. The far target is 45 feet to 50 feet away from the center of the edge of the casting box. The other three targets are set at random distances between the nearest and the farthest but not in a straight line, perpendicular to the casting box.

### Tackle

The rod shall not be more than 9 feet, 6 inches long. The reel is unrestricted. The line can be any weight, but not marked in terms of distances or attached at the reel at the 50-foot mark. The single-strand leader cannot be less than 6 feet in length. The fly must be an official ACA dry fly. The hackle of the fly shall not be less than 3/4" or more than 1 inch in diameter. The fly cannot be oiled or treated in any way.

### Time

The caster has eight (8) minutes to complete the Dry Fly Event. Time starts after he/she enters the casting box. Ten presentation casts are made to the targets in order or as designated by the captain of the event (two rounds of five each). Only one hand on the rod.

### Method of Casting

The caster begins with fly in hand and no more than the leader plus two feet of line extending beyond the tip. Caster may make as many false casts to any targets within the 8-minute time limit. The false cast is the mechanism in which the line, leader, and fly are moved through the air without intentionally striking the surface in front of the casting box. The cast is completed when the fly, leader, or line settles on the water on a final forward delivery. The caster must not pick up the fly in preparation for the next target until the judge calls "score."

### Scoring and Penalties
A perfect score (100 points) consists of ten casts where the fly falls within or hits any part of the target. For each foot or fraction of a foot missed one (1) demerit is charged. All demerits are subtracted from the score. Maximum demerits for any single final forward cast shall be five (5).

Penalties of three (3) demerits can be charged for each of the following: Sunken fly, tick, improper strip, improper retrieve, improper cast and overtime (for each minute or fraction thereof beyond the allotted eight minutes). Three demerits are charged if the caster starts with more than two feet of line and leader beyond the rod tip.

**PENALTY DEFINITIONS:** *Sunken Fly*—If the fly fails to float, or sinks and rises to the surface, on a final forward cast; *Improper Strip*—If the caster strips line from the reel or pulls line in through the guides while the fly is on the surface in front of the casting box and the rod is not in motion in the act of making a cast; *Improper Retrieve*—If the caster lifts the fly from the water after a final forward cast before the Judge calls "Score;" *Improper Cast*—If the caster allows the fly to dangle or to be blown over a target: *Tick*—If the fly strikes the water during a false cast.

# TROUT FLY ACCURACY

### Target Course
The targets are 30-inch diameter rings and set in water. The nearest target is 20 to 25 feet from the center of the edge of the casting box. The far target is 45 feet to 50 feet away from the center of the edge of the casting box. The other three targets

are set at random distances between the nearest and the farthest but not in a straight line, perpendicular to the casting box.

## Tackle
The rod cannot be longer than 9 feet. The reel is unrestricted. The line must be a standard plastic floating line in a 6 weight (not to exceed 0.053") and not marked to indicate distance. The leader cannot be less than 9 feet. The leader tippet must be at least 18 inches long and must not exceed .008" in diameter. The fly must be an official ACA trout fly. The hackle shall not exceed one-half (1/2) inch in diameter.

## Time
The caster has six (6) minutes to complete the course of the three rounds (Dry Fly, Wet Fly and Roll Cast) or 15 targets. Time begins with the first presentation cast in the Dry Fly Round.

## FIRST ROUND - DRY FLY

### Method of Casting
Casting one handed (one hand on the rod), the caster makes one presentation (scoring) cast to each of the five targets, starting with the closest. The caster may make as many false casts as he/she would like, bearing in mind that there is a 6-minute time limit for all three rounds. The false cast in which the line, leader, and fly are moved through the air without intentionally striking the surface in front of the casting box is the mechanism for letting line out and measuring distance to the next target. The caster must not pick up the fly in preparation for the next target until the judge calls "score."

### Scoring and Penalties
A fly falling within or on any portion of the target on a final forward cast shall be scored a perfect. There is one (1) demerit assessed for each foot or fraction the fly misses the target on a final forward cast. Maximum demerits for any single final forward cast shall be two (2).

Penalties of one (1) demerit can be charged for the following: sunken fly, ticks, improper strip, improper retrieve, and improper cast (allowing the wind to dangle the fly over a target). Two (2) demerits for failure to begin with fly in hand.

## SECOND ROUND - WET FLY

### Method of Casting

The caster retrieves the line without placing it on the reel and begins with fly in hand and no more than leader plus 2 feet of line extending beyond the rod tip. The caster then false casts as many times as required before the final forward cast to the nearest target. Caster must not hold coiled line in hand before or during cast to the nearest target.

After the first target the caster goes to the next nearest target and through to all five. Line must be extended only while the fly is in the air. Only one (1) false cast is allowed between targets two (2) through five (5).

### Scoring and Penalties

For each foot or fraction the fly misses the target on a final forward cast, a demerit of one (1) is assessed. Maximum demerits are two (2).

Penalties of one (1) demerit can be charged for each of the following: tick, improper strip, improper retrieve or additional false cast. Two (2) demerits for failure to begin with fly in hand. *(See Penalty Definitions in Dry Fly Accuracy.)*

## THIRD ROUND - ROLL CAST

### Method of Casting

A roll cast is defined as one in which the fly does not intentionally leave the water until the rod is in the deliberate forward motion. The round consists of no more than fifteen (15) roll casts at the target course.

After completing the Wet Fly round, the caster strips the line in to measure the closest target. The fly remains on the water. The caster then roll casts to the first target (which counts as the first roll cast) and continues until a perfect is scored and then proceeds to the next nearest target and so on. A caster remains on a target until it is hit. A maximum of 15 roll casts is allowed.

### Scoring and Penalties

False casting is not permitted and a penalty of two (2) demerits shall be assessed. Two (2) demerits shall be assessed for each target not hit within the allocated fifteen (15) roll casts or if time expires.

The caster's score is 100 points less the total number of demerits for accuracy and for penalties from the three rounds.

# BASS BUG ACCURACY

### Target Course

There are six targets, which include the same five used in Dry Fly and Trout Fly, plus a sixth target set out at least 65 feet but not more than 70 feet. The nearest, second farthest and farthest targets are in line with the center of the casting box, but the other three targets are randomly placed as per the Dry Fly or Trout Fly Events.

### Tackle

The rod cannot be more than 9 ft. 3/4 in. long. The reel is unrestricted. The line must be a floating type with a maximum diameter not exceeding .068 inches. The leader cannot be less than 6 feet with a tippet not less than 12 inches that does not exceed .014 inch in diameter. The bass bug must be an official ACA bass bug.

### Time

Time starts when the bass bug is placed on the water from the first presentation cast of the first round. The caster has five (5) minutes to complete the two rounds (total 12 targets).

## FIRST ROUND - BASS BUG
### Method of Casting

The line shall be stripped from the reel by the caster or judge and the bug placed at least ten feet beyond the farthest target. The caster retrieves the line by stripping it in (but not wound on reel) and begins with bug in hand and no more than the leader plus two feet of line extending beyond the tip. The caster may false cast as many times as required to measure distance to the nearest target before making the first presentation (and scored) cast. The caster shall proceed to the next nearest target and so on until all six targets have been cast using no more than two false casts.

## SECOND ROUND - BASS BUG

### Method of Casting

At the conclusion of the sixth final forward cast (to the farthest target) in Round One, the caster shall retrieve the line by stripping in (but not wound on the reel). The caster begins with bug in hand and no more than two (2) feet of line extended beyond the tip of the rod. The caster shall repeat the procedure of Round One except that only one (1) false cast shall be allowed between targets two through six.

### Scoring and Penalties

A perfect score of 100 points consists of 12 casts where the bug falls within or hits any part of the target. For each foot or fraction of a foot missed one (1) demerit is charged. A maximum demerit of two (2) shall be called for targets one through five. Target six shall have a maximum demerit of five (5).

Penalties of one (1) demerit are charged for each tick or extra false casts. Exception: Unlimited number of false casts on first target is allowed.  A penalty of two (2) demerits is charged for failing to begin either round with bass bug in hand and more than two feet of line and leader beyond the rod tip.

# FLY DISTANCE EVENTS

There are three fly distance events: Angler's Fly Distance, One-Hand Fly Distance, and Two-Hand Fly Distance

## ANGLER'S FLY DISTANCE

### Tackle

The rod cannot be longer than 9-ft., 1-in. long. The reel is unrestricted but must be attached to the rod and be capable of holding the entire line. The line, a shooting head, shall be no longer than 31 feet in length and no shorter than 28 feet and weigh no more than 310 grains. The running line is unrestricted except that the diameter shall not be less than 0.015 inches. The leader must not be less than 9 feet or longer than 12 feet. The fly is the official ACA fly with hackle not smaller than 5/8-inch in diameter.

*Course and Method of Casting*
The course shall be of sufficient length and shall consist of a court that is a maximum of 180 degrees wide. Casting is done one handed (only one hand on rod) with a total casting time of five minutes with as many casts as the caster desires in the allotted time. Time-outs are allowed only for outside interference. The caster may have assistance in removing line from reel and in straightening line, during the preparation time. During the event, the caster shall be allowed no further assistance.

### Scoring
The distance of the cast is measured from the casting box to the point where the fly lands within the boundaries of the court. The caster's longest shooting cast shall constitute the caster's score. The caster's second longest cast is recorded in case of a tie.

# ONE-HAND FLY DISTANCE

### Tackle
The rod cannot exceed 9-ft., 9-in. in length. The reel is unrestricted but must be attached to the rod and capable of holding the entire line. The line, a shooting head, cannot be less than 49-ft., 3-in. and cannot weigh more than 650 grains. The running line is unrestricted. The leader cannot be longer than 12 feet or shorter than 6 feet in length. The fly must be an official ACA fly. The hackle of the fly shall not be smaller than 5/8-inch in diameter.

### Course and Method of Casting
The course shall be of sufficient length and shall consist of a court that is a maximum of 180 degrees. The casting is done one handed (only one hand on the rod) with a total casting time of five minutes with as many casts as the caster desires during

the allotted time. Time-outs are allowed only for outside interference. One assistant (ghillie) is allowed with the caster to tend line or generally assist the caster.

*Scoring*

The distance of the cast is measured from the box to the point where the fly lands within the boundaries of the court. The caster's longest shooting cast shall constitute the caster's score. The caster's second longest cast is recorded in case of a tie.

# TWO-HAND FLY DISTANCE

*Tackle*

The rod cannot be more than 17 feet long. The reel is unrestricted but must be attached to the rod and be capable of holding the entire line. The line, a shooting head, is unrestricted except the weight shall not exceed 1855 grains. The running line is unrestricted. The leader shall not be longer than 17 feet or shorter than 6 feet in length. The fly must be an official ACA fly. The hackle of the fly shall not be smaller than 5/8-inch in diameter.

*Course and Method of Casting*

The course shall be of sufficient length and consist of a court that is a maximum of 180 degrees. Casting is two handed (two hands on rod) with a time of seven minutes with as many casts as the caster desires during the allotted time. Time-outs are allowed only for outside interference. One assistant (ghillie) is allowed with the caster to tend line or generally assist the caster.

*Scoring*

The distance of the cast is measured from the box to the point where the fly lands within the boundaries of the court. The caster's longest shooting cast shall constitute the caster's score. The caster's second longest cast is recorded in case of a tie.

**For more specific rules or changes log on to**

*http://www.americancastingassoc.org*

# The 5-Weight Fly Distance Event

THIS NEW DISTANCE FLY-CASTING EVENT is attracting considerable interest and publicity. Instead of using the heavy tackle associated with the ACA distance fly games, this event is limited to a 5-weight forward taper floating line and off-the-rack 5-weight, 9-foot rods. By standardizing the equipment, everyone starts from a level playing field insofar as the tackle is concerned.

Much of the 5-weight's popularity stems from the fact that the International Sportsmen's Exposition (ISE) features this event at its popular sport shows that take place in six western cities during the first four months of the year. Billed as *The Best In the West,* this casting competition has stirred considerable interest and curiosity among anglers and some tournament casters. The 5-weight is not an ACA event.

Because the tackle used in this event resembles the fishing gear that one could expect to see on streams, many anglers have been attracted to this game. The competition among the top casters is fierce, more so because there are usually some very expensive prizes for the winner.

It usually takes a cast of about 110 feet to win the 5-weight men's division. That's quite a cast. In the three ACA distance fly events, thin, high density shooting heads are used (which cut through the air faster), and the running lines consist of fine diameter monofilament instead of the thicker "slower" fly line.

As I've mentioned elsewhere in this book, many anglers think they cast farther than they do, because they generally do not measure their casts with a tape measure (stepping it off is usually inaccurate). If an angler casts out a full 90-ft. line, he concludes that his casting distance is 90 feet plus the length of the leader. Casts are measured from the angler to where the fly lands, not by how much line off the reel. It's downright frustrating to have made that gloriously long cast, with many yards of line shooting through the guides, only to discover that about three (or more!) yards of line plus the leader fell back in loose coils. Getting the line and leader to straighten out is one of the vexing problems, not only in the 5-weight but in all distance fly events.

To be in the winner's circle, in the 5-weight men's division, the caster will probably have to carry (false cast) about 75 to 85 feet of line and then shoot the rest. It's not easy to aerialize 80 feet of line and to develop sufficient speed and a very tight loop to shoot out the additional line. Highly skilled casters, who can easily cast 160 feet with tournament gear, have trouble casting the 5-weight, because the stroke and timing is different.

A 5-weight distance fly cult has developed and includes such high priests as Rick Hartman, Jim Gunderson, Lance Egan, Clay Roberts, Brian O'Keefe, Jerry Siem, Bill Gammel, Jeff Wagner, Randy Swisher and others. The Rajeff brothers, Steve and Tim, represent the tournament casters very well and have won a number of contests. The Revel teenage brothers have also won in the 5-weight distance tournaments.

Let's look at some of the rules and tackle used in the 2005 ISE Best in the West fly casting competition:

**ADULT DIVISION RULES:**
The contest is for distance only. Qualifying distance for men is 90 feet; for women, 65 feet. Competitors have three casts to achieve maximum distance. One warm-up cast is allowed; competitor can keep the warm-up cast if he/she requests to have

it measured. If contestant keeps the warm-up cast, he or she has two remaining casts.

Length of cast is determined by where the fly lands. Fly must land within the confines of the casting pond. A fly that goes "out of bounds" will not be recorded but counts as one of the three attempts. If the fly comes off, it is a redo. Contestant stepping over starting marker will have that cast disallowed. All casting must be completed within five minutes.

**YOUTH DIVISION RULES:**
Contestants 14 and under are eligible for the Youth Division. Qualifying Distance: 35 ft. Rules are similar to the Adult Division.

**GEAR**
(Competitors choose from one of the three rod and reel combinations):

*Rod:* Sage TCR 590-4 (9 ft., 5 wt., 4 piece); *Reel:* Sage 3300 reel.

*Rod:* G. Loomis Streamdance GLX (9 ft., 5 wt., 4 piece) *Reel:* G. Loomis Syncrotech.

*Rod:* Scott S3 (9 ft., 5 wt., 4 piece) *Reel:* G. Loomis Syncrotech.

*Line:* Scientific Anglers XXD COMP 125 ft. WF-5-F

*Leader:* Scientific Anglers Mastery Series, 9 ft., 0X, 10 lb.

Here are the scores that determined the 2005 grand champions held at the Salt Lake City, Utah sport show:

**Men's Division:**
Champion: Rick Hartman: 111' 9"
Runner-up: Jim Gunderson: 106' 9"

**Women's Division:**
Champion: Wendy Gunn: 86' 5"
Runner-Up: Sandi Roberts: 79' 10"

The Grand Prize for each division (Men's and Women's) was a paid fishing trip (including air transportation) to Argentina for 4½ days guided fishing, hotels, transfers, etc. Value=$4,000.

In the Utah State Championship for Youth (14 or under) the

winners were: 1st Place: Eric Merizon: 75' 3"; 2nd Place: Towson Jenkins: 65' 8"; 3rd Place: Austin Hatfield: 60' 7." From what I've heard, the longest cast in actual competition is 119 ft. I understand that Rick Hartman has thrown casts into the mid-120s, witnessed by Bruce Richards, a superb caster/ angler. Rick has cast in practice over 130 ft. according to witnesses. Bruce works for Scientific Anglers, which manufactures the official line for *The Best in the West* and other competitions.

The 5-weight distance fly is not confined to the ISE sport shows, and similar tournaments have been elsewhere.

The Outdoor Life Network (OLN) produced its popular *Fly Fishing Masters* for the past three seasons (now cancelled). Competitors vying for $52,000 in prize money had to compete in distance and accuracy casting events using a 5-weight line and rod. Through a series of casting competitions in various parts of the country, winning teams of two persons competed in stream fishing to determine the winner. Tournament casters Steve and Tim Rajeff won the 2002 first place ($30,000) not only because of their incredible casting skills, but also because of their rich, varied fishing experiences and background, which includes guiding.

ESPN's *The Great Outdoor Games* also has a similar contest that combines distance and accuracy casting and features a fishing competition on a trout stream.

Across the pond, the British Fly Casting Club, only a few years in existence, offers the 5-weight distance competition for its members. At the time of this writing, Carl Hutchinson holds the club record with a cast of 116 ft. 8 in., while Mike Marshall's 105 ft. 2 in. cast is the Senior's record.

While the ISE's *The Best of the West* competition is held indoors at the sport shows, all the other major competitions take place outdoors.

No doubt about it: The 5-weight distance is here to stay. It's being cast at a number of fly-fishing club outings.

I wondered whether the 5-weight is the best possible line size for a more universally accepted distance event by anglers. My reasoning is that if an angler is using a 5-weight, he is probably fishing smaller rivers and confined streams where casts are limited in distance because of brush, trees and other obstacles. Perhaps a 7-weight event would be more popular and address fishing situations that require long casts better. (The English BFCC has a 7-weight event as well as the 5 weight.)

But proponents of the 5-weight aren't interested in changes. They love the game. Besides, on many lakes a longer cast is often necessary so as not to spook fish, and many western rivers dictate longer casts. Good point.

***Long live the 5-weight!***

# S E C T I O N   T H R E E

THE BENEFITS OF PRACTICE CASTING include: better fishing results; the sheer pleasure derived from fly casting itself; and, it's a healthy, wholesome activity that can be enjoyed by friends and family members.

The degree of participation depends on the individual. One person may enjoy casting at targets or for distance strictly for personal satisfaction; another person may wish to enter competition at various tournament levels. The choice is yours. At the minimum,  casting is a wonderful fill-in activity between fishing trips.

In this section you'll learn how you can use your video camera to improve your casting. We'll visit with Steve Rajeff (no one has dominated his sport more than Steve has). Then we'll chat with Dick Fujita and other casters to get various perspectives. Dr. Sam Davis tell us how he successfully launched the British Fly Casting Club.

You'll also learn more about starting a casting club, hosting a tournament and why casting is truly a family activity— one that can be enjoyed by all ages, from preteen to the over-80 crowd.

And, finally, my confessions about my addiction.

# Improve your casting
# the video way

IF YOU ARE SERIOUS about improving your casting (and I'm sure you are if you've read this far!), how about videotaping your casting progress from time to time? Golfers, baseball, basketball and football players, divers and just about anyone involved in athletics use video equipment extensively.

Why not casters? It's relatively easy to do, and who can resist seeing themselves casting on television or a computer monitor? Many of the top casters use electronic media to help evaluate their casting.

Most of us have a fair knowledge of what a good casting stroke should look like but when we are casting we obviously can't see our stroke, loops or rod paths.

It's easy. Set up a video camera on a tripod, aim and focus the camera on the area where you will be casting, press the record button and start your casting. The problem is that, unless you have a remote control that can work at some distance, you will also record the time you spend stripping in the line from one of your fabulous casts. This is time consuming. It's best to enlist the services of a friend or family member.

Whether you are shooting your own tape, or someone else is doing it, you should record your casts from various angles: Front, back and from each side. You'll want some close-ups as well as some distant shots. Try to do your taping with a plain background, such as sky, so that hopefully you can see the loops, rod path, and stroke, trajectory and timing.

Randy Olson, a lifelong angler who became interested in tournament casting just a few years ago, has used the video camera to develop into one of our best young casters. He gives credit to the video camera for much of his progress.

"Because I live in the 'desert' of eastern Montana—Golden Gate in San Francisco is the nearest casting club—I knew I would have to videotape myself to see my flaws and hopefully correct them," Randy explains. "I knew how to analyze casting strokes of others; however, analyzing yourself is a little different story, because you can't see yourself casting. Some of the casting gurus at the Federation of Fly Fishers conventions and other fly fishing shows recommended videotaping one's casting.

"So that is what I did. I would tape from the front, back and each side. The front to back is most revealing in terms of how your rod is tracking in the vertical plane. The side view really shows your trajectory, and with a good camera and the right background, the path of your rod tip. The rod tip must travel in a straight line, period. Casting a shooting head really seems to magnify all of your flaws, so I believe just practicing these events makes you a better caster."

After taping a session you can view the tape on your television set by connecting the camera to it, but I prefer to use a VCR, because I can easily arrange to "fast forward" or reverse certain critical segments of my casting. I can view sections in slow motion for more critical analysis.

I like to view a tape after I cast because I'm curious; however, the best time is to study it just before your next session so that any casting flaws that need correcting are fresh in your memory.

Are you stopping the rod abruptly at critical times? What about your double haul? Is your "hauling" hand extending all the way back *a lá* Rajeff or Korich on your distance casting?

While the video camera becomes particularly important to the distance fly caster, it is also very useful for the angler who wants to improve his accuracy. Is he using too much wrist? Is there too much slack on his back cast? What about tailing loops or very wide loops? Much can be learned with the aid of a video camera for casters interested in distance or accuracy casting.

If you don't have a video camera, but have a digital camera that has a movie-making feature, you can use it, but because most digital cameras only record a short duration (10 to 20 seconds) it is not as convenient or as effective.

# Between casts with Steve Rajeff

I T WAS ONE OF those great trout days on Alaska's Goodnews River. I was fishing with Bob Stearns, who for many years wrote for *Field and Stream*. Nevin, our guide, stressed the importance of casting our mouse imitations right against the bank. Nevin was right. Casts that landed a couple of feet away were usually ignored; however, if the mouse landed a few inches from the bank, it usually was engulfed by a feisty rainbow. The cast had to be precise.

During shore lunch, our talk turned to casting. It was obvious that Nevin knew a lot about casting. In the off season, he worked at a Montana fly shop and often taught fly casting.

"One day, at the store," Nevin told us, "the boss asked me to teach this young guy to fly cast quickly, because he was taking a number of important business prospects on a fishing trip. The fellow seemed athletic and pleasant. I've taught many people the fundamentals of fly casting fairly quickly, so this should be a piece of cake.

"I demonstrated. I explained. Over and over again. The fellow was one of the most uncoordinated students I've ever had. He just couldn't get the hang of it. I excused myself, and went into the store and told the boss that this guy is hopeless.

"The boss tells me I gotta teach him. He is buying lots of fly-fishing outfits for this business entertainment trout fishing trip.

"The boss was getting impatient. So he came out and said he would teach the fellow to cast. First he stripped all the line from the reel because it was loose. He left all the line on the ground. The boss makes a couple of false casts and drops the fly about 35 feet. 'That's all you have to do. Now you try it,' the boss said and hands the rod to the student.

"The fellow takes the rod and says, 'You mean like this?' and makes a couple of false casts and on the third forward cast he adds a double haul and the entire fly line shoots out through the guides, yanks at the reel, and this is the most perfect, the longest cast I have ever seen in my life!

"I was stunned. I was shocked. Then they both broke into laughter. The fellow turned out to be Steve Rajeff, world casting champion for many years. The boss put him up to it, and Steve did a great job of pretending not to be able to cast." During the afternoon fishing session, I chuckled several times thinking about that story.

I had not met Steve at the time Nevin told me the story, but I have since then on numerous occasions at tournaments. He has always been very helpful and shares information readily even with his top competitors.

Steve won the ACA All-Round Casting Championships in 1972 when he was 15 years old. He has won the All-Round title 32 times and was co-champion twice (with Chris Korich and Henry Mittel). He won the World All-Round Casting title 13 times out of the 17 times he competed. An incredible accomplishment! Besides casting, Steve is one of the finest all-round light-tackle anglers today. I recently interviewed him between his casting tournaments and fishing trips:

**Q: Steve, I know you excel in every casting event, but what's your favorite fly event?**

SR: My favorite event is Single-Hand Fly Distance. It takes a combination of excellent technique and strength to make it really cast far. It has been my best event at national and world competitions.

**Q: What advice would you give a person who is interested in becoming a better caster—obviously practice more, but anything additional?**

SR: To get better at any sport, the wise athletes and competitors get a trainer or coach. In fly casting, the best casters get lessons from a casting instructor. There are many good fly casting instructors now, and they can be located on a list from the Federation of Fly Fishers. Also, you can check in at your local fly-fishing shop. Many fly-fishing guides are excellent casting instructors, as well. However, when fishing, it is often difficult to concentrate purely on casting, so I suggest practice before trips.

**Q: What are your thoughts on the 5-Weight Distance Fly Event that's gaining some popularity?**

SR: The event is like trying to throw a ping-pong ball the farthest. The line is relatively light and air resistant. It is a game of hand speed and tight loops. He who has the fastest hands and can make a tight loop, which generates the highest line speed, should win. It is an easy event to do, but difficult to do really well. Most casters struggle with making a very narrow loop on the back cast. The longer the line you may aerialize, the longer the cast may go. The key to aerializing a lot of line is having a very tight loop in the back cast. It is a good event because most people already have a 5-weight outfit.

**Q: What's your favorite fish—or several species—that you enjoy or find challenging?**

SR: I enjoy many species when conditions are right. Among my favorite are steelhead, bonefish, permit, tarpon, trout, Atlantic salmon, yellowfin tuna and barracuda. Seeking any one of these fish can take you to beautiful places and, when the situation is right, can totally captivate your focus and attention, blocking out life's mundane obligations. I have been fortunate to travel to some of the best places for some of these species and would gladly go back there again.

**Q: What is your practicing regime. Do you practice or just cast in tournaments?**

SR: As a young caster growing up in San Francisco, I would go to the Golden Gate Angling and Casting Club almost every day after school, as well as on weekends. I would practice casting while other kids played ball. In preparing for a major competition, I would practice eight weeks with a plan. I would concentrate on events that were my weakest first, lightly practicing my strong events. I would be careful not to get blisters, or any other injuries. Practice time would range about one to three hours every day. About five days before the competition, I would stop casting to give all the muscles, tendons, and ligaments a chance to rest, and concentrate on getting the tackle all ready for the competitions.

**Q: What do you think is necessary to improve the popularity of casting?**

SR: Prize money and public recognition are the keys to the development of any other sport and a key to developing casting. The reason the 5-weight fly distance events have gained interest is because they are held at sportsmen's shows, typically with a significant prize for the winners: A trip to Argentina, a drift boat, prize money and publicity in fly-fishing publications. There are many casters trying to reinvent the games we cast in competition, but I doubt many more people will try the events unless there is something more to gain than a small medal and recognition by the other casters only.

**Q: Which of the many casting accomplishments are you most proud of?**

SR: My personal best cast was during the World Casting Championships in Pretoria, South Africa held in 1998. In the Single-Hand Fly Distance Event, I managed a personal best cast of 248 feet and won the event by over 10 feet. The winds were swirling, and mostly from right to left. For about

 the time to make three casts, the wind was down court, and I managed a perfect loop and trajectory. I did it with as much power as I could apply, considering a lot of lower back pain from a compressed disc pinching on a nerve. The cast was not an official record. There is a wind meter for international competitions, and the maximum wind speed for setting a record is 3 meters per second (about 8

mph). Although the caster on another court next to me placed second and was 10 feet shorter, they granted him the official record, for whatever reason.

**Q: What's your best fishing accomplishment?**

SR: Among my most memorable fishing accomplishments was catching a giant tarpon while fishing with my friend Ted Juracsik, maker of Tibor reels. He took me snook fishing in the Everglades, and we spotted a tarpon roll. He suggested changing flies to a larger black one, with a heavier shock tippet. As we approached the area we saw the tarpon roll again, and I let go a 75-foot cast with the 9-weight outfit I was using for snook. On the third strip, the rod was nearly pulled out of my hands and a giant tarpon jumped about 70 feet away. It was huge. Ted laughed and said we are in for it now. With all the pressure the tackle would stand, we had the tarpon near to the boat within 30 minutes, following several long runs and jumps. Ted had poled about a half mile to keep up with the fish. When we were ready to land the tarpon, I asked Ted if he had a lip gaff. He said he did not have his lip gaff because we were snook fishing.

We tried to lasso the tail with a slip noose off the end of the push pole, but that only scared the fish. Finally Ted instructed me to wind the leader all the way to the rod tip, and lift like hell. As I lifted as high as possible, he reached out as far as he could, and promptly fell overboard. This really scared the big fish, and it swam off in one direction, leaving Ted treading water in another. He yelled out to get the boat over to him right away, because, in the murky water, it was hard to see sharks. Bull sharks are very common in the area, and prone to eating your tired tarpon at the final stage of the fight. I gave a lot of slack in the line, put the rod under my arm, grabbed the push pole, and moved the boat closer to Ted. I staked out the pole with a rope to the poling platform, and regained tension on the line and was delighted to feel the fish was still on. I worked the fish close enough for Ted to wrap his arms around the fish and guide the head to me at the bow of the skiff. I grabbed the lip and slid the giant fish onboard.

It was a miracle. The fish was nearly seven feet long, and bigger around than my 40-inch waist. We conservatively estimated her to weigh 170 pounds.

**Q: Steve, despite your having won so many casting championships and having fished for most of the important game fish, your passion for the next casting tournament or fishing trip is very evident.**

*(Steve smiled as he prepared for his next steelhead trip.)*

# Between casts with Dick Fujita

I ONCE ASKED STEVE RAJEFF about casting lessons. "You want to become a good caster? Go find Dick Fujita. He knows what casting is all about." Coming from Steve— probably the best caster ever—it's a wonderful tribute to Dick Fujita. This 79-year-old competitor continues to WOW! people with his smooth casting delivery and outstanding accomplishments.

**Q: Dick, what's your favorite fly event?**
DF: The Dry Fly Event. The nature of this game places a premium on executing a consistent and controlled false cast. It's possible that an individual could execute as many as 100 casts in order to complete the game. In past years, my Dry Fly accuracy practice session often consisted of five consecutive games, so 500 false casts in a session was not unreasonable. This type of practice session contributes to the development of hand and arm muscles, timing, loop control, line manipulation and a more conscious appreciation of the value of controlled power intensity and controlled relaxation.

Now when I'm fishing, I never make more than two false casts. I remove moisture from the dry fly on the back cast, because I found doing so on a forward cast tends to spray over the fish and this can alert wary species like trout.

The Trout Fly and Bass Bug Events have their place as attractor games, but they do not afford the same conditioning opportunity that the Dry Fly game does. Personally, I have better adapted to stream fishing situations through the Dry Fly Event than from the Trout Fly game.

The Trout Fly Event is a progressive near-to-far target order game. Line manipulation is not as critical. The event is timed and there is no pure "Dry Fly" delivery involved. A "speed" casting game has its place in the pure competitive aspects although it becomes nothing more than a wet fly event. Sooner or later, the next generation will probably sway the casters into using a higher speed, small-diameter line.

**Q: What's your favorite distance fly event?**
DF: The Single Hand Fly Distance Event with the Two-Hand Distance game a close second. The Single Hand requires a bit more conditioning, coordination and analytical appraisal of casting than any of the other fly events. At 5 feet, 6 inches and weighing 148 to 152 pounds, I do not expect to throw astronomical distances, but I feel I should cast as much as I weigh. Some time ago, when I weighed 125 pounds, using an 8-ounce Winston bamboo rod and silk fly line, I did throw 172 feet at a regional tournament. I lost by one foot!

Despite my gaining weight and the development of lighter and faster tip rods and slick lines, my distance plateau is at a lower level today. It's got to be the unfavorable atmospheric conditions—not aging. Don't you think?

**Q: [Chuckle...] How about the Two-Hand Fly Distance Event?**
DF: I do have the opportunity to occasionally practice it and I am mired at the 195- to 215-foot range. I have always felt that I should throw in the 230- to 235-foot bracket.

Back in the bamboo rod era, when a Winston 15-foot rod weighed more than two pounds and we cast on water, it was virtually impossible for me to handle such an outfit with any degree of success. I didn't want to give up this event so I made a semi-hollow cedar core 15-foot rod using a Herter's form. The rod weighed 1 pound 4 ounces and I was able to throw 20 to 25 feet farther than with the heavier rod and with reasonably good form.

The distance fly games are for heavyweights. Six-foot tall

casters with long arm spans. It's difficult for me to execute more than two false casts prior to final delivery. Therefore, the execution of the first pickup for the back cast is of primary importance. The challenge is ever present!

**Q: It's amazing what you've been able to do. You prove that timing and line control are the keys. I heard that you've lost some sight in one eye and yet you are a very accurate caster.**

DF: I almost lost an eye when the salmon [Two-Hand Fly Distance] leader during a cast wound around my head and the heavy #6 hook slammed into my left eyeglass lens. This was one year before the government forced manufacturers to produce shatterproof lenses. The impact sprayed bits of glass into my eyes. It was fortunate that I ended up with a scratched cornea and not the retina. I am not blind in that eye although some of my scores may dispute that. I cast that year in the National tournament with an eye patch.

**Q: And you have a pacemaker?**

DF: I've had a pacemaker since 1985. Battery life depends on technology and usage demand. My first pacemaker lasted nearly ten years. A new improved model lasted six years and my current one is three years old. So far, all operations occurred during the casting "off-season," so it has not put me out of tournament casting action.

I have received some precautionary advice discouraging strenuous physical activity requiring arm and shoulder usage. The possibility of loosening the attachment to the battery has been mentioned; however, none of the tournament distance games have caused any problem.

The primary reason for the implant was because of a skipping heartbeat that tends to restrict oxygen to the brain, which causes seizure.

The only problem that comes to mind, prior to installation of the pacemaker, is when I was wading the Boyne River in Michigan. At that time I could not recall how I managed to be upright and then in the next instant found myself on my knees in the water. However, I managed to keep the rod and reel dry. I must have had a mild seizure and was fortunate enough to be fishing a shallow part of the stream. I should mention that there was a huge Chinook salmon on the end of the line.

**Q: I believe your dad got you interested in tournament casting. Did you like casting from the beginning, or did casting grow on you?**

DF: My dad was a tournament surf caster and striped bass fisherman before he was introduced to the fly and plug casting games at San Francisco's Golden Gate Angling and Casting Club. I was not permitted to fish with him until I learned to cast. I started with plug casting around 1936.

My first fishing trip was in 1938. I was 12. I had a bamboo rod and a Shakespeare free spool 1740 reel. I caught two largemouth bass. The biggest was six pounds. I was more attracted to tournament casting than to fishing because I did not feel that crescendo of excitement that one reads about in fishing literature. Peggy Lee's "Is That All There Is" philosophical song probably best expresses how I felt at the time.

I was not permitted to cast a fly rod until I was 14 and I remember my first casting tournament at Turlock, California. I cast 93 percent. In those days, the delicate delivery of the dry fly was very much in vogue and a perfect score was difficult to attain.

From those early years, Pop often stressed that in order to maintain a lasting participation and interest in tournament casting I should compete in all the events. He was absolutely correct.

**Q: Do you recall your first trout trip and other fishing trips?**
DF: The first trip was on the famous Au Sable River in Michigan around 1953. The first fish was so small that I "false cast" it accidentally. But I did catch a 16-inch trout on that trip.

In the early 1970s, I did reduce my tournament casting and ventured into the Pennsylvania streams experimenting with various rods from 6 to 8 feet in length.

I then fished in Michigan where the streams were a little wider, but again, Peggy Lee's haunting "Is That All There Is" kept popping up.

I fished Montana's Bitterroot River, as luck would have it, during a severe drought. I landed three trout with no more than 15 feet of line. Again Peggy Lee.

I fished in Florida for bonefish and tarpon during very windy conditions. I caught a bonefish that ran three times before tiring. Peggy Lee's song again.

Steelhead fishing around Cleveland and Pennsylvania is as good as anywhere in the country. I live only about 15 minutes from a good river that is loaded with steelhead. Unfortunately casting perfection is not a required dimension for success.

I met George Harvey, the professor of Angling Arts at Penn State and his assistant Joe Humphries. Fishing experts are always trying to size up a tournament caster's proficiency on the stream. After our trip upstream, George complimented me and said that I had all the moves to become the greatest fly fisherman! His flattering comment surprised me because I don't recall doing anything extraordinary other than adjusting to conditions.

*Q: That's quite an honor coming from one of the best trout fishermen of all time. Back to casting. What advice would you give a novice caster to improve his fly-casting accuracy in competition?*

DF: Be aware of the size of the loop and behavior of the line and leader, because it must straighten and hover over the target during the false cast. The hover type of cast is different from the more natural "continuous stroked" cast. The hover cast requires an abrupt hit on the forward cast followed by complete relaxation. The back cast needs to be powerful with maximum lift and flip followed by a relaxed grip. It's the relaxed grip after application of controlled power intensity that helps propel the line with maximum speed. Of course, different rod actions will dictate the stroke length and application of power intensity. I know that this advice doesn't conform to some of the "how-to" casting articles.

**Q: How much time do you devote to practice casting?**
DF: I do not have the opportunity to practice accuracy as often as I wish. Actual practice occurs at registered tournaments these days. I try to practice the distance events on open weekends if the field is not occupied by Little Leaguers. During my early years I would practice on Saturday or Sunday or both starting at 9:30 a.m. and packing it in at 5 or 6 p.m. No lunch. No water. Old age and improved judgment has changed my hours to practicing from about 3:30 p.m. to 6:30 p.m.

**Q: What do you think is your best single accomplishment in tournaments?**
DF: It's difficult to pinpoint a single best. Perhaps it would be the Lexington, Kentucky 2004 Tournament, which was my 56th National. I've competed in 50 consecutive Nationals since 1955. And, of course, being inducted into the ACA Hall of Fame and the International Casting Hall of Fame are at the top of the list.

**Q: Where were you born and what do you do to stay fit?**
DF: Well, I was born in 1926, in Napa, California. In those years, Napa was not known for its wine; its claim to fame was an insane asylum! I'm 5 feet 6 inches and gradually shrinking and weigh about 150 to 153 pounds in the summer. I am not a physical fitness addict—I get my exercise from casting. Occasionally, I lift light dumbbells for short periods of time. And I don't count calories.

***Q: Well, Dick, I know of many of your outstanding casting accomplishments. You are truly a wonderful ambassador for casting, as is your brother Henry. And, of course, your dad, Henry Fujita Sr. was a tremendous contributor to the sport of casting.***

# The BFCC: where distance is a way of life!

C ARL HUTCHINSON cast 198 ft. in the Single-Hand Fly Distance Event. Scott Simmonds threw a fly 256 ft. in the Two-Hand Fly Distance, while 68-year-old Mike Marshall's cast measured an incredible 248 feet! In an event similar to the ACA's Angler's Fly, James Warbrick-Smith cast 171 feet! These great casts did not take place at a West Coast casting club known for some of the greatest distance casters in history, but instead in England at a club that's only two years old.

The club was formed by Dr. Sam Davis, who was born in Japan, raised in South Carolina, educated in England (earning his doctorate in Evolutionary Biology from University College, London), and now lives and works in Brittany, France as a professional fishing guide, lodge co-owner and outfitter. (Web site: *www.fishandfunbrittany.com* )
In late 2002, Sam developed a strong interest in tournament casting. He was living in England at the time, and in mid-2003 he founded the British Fly Casting Club (BFCC). In a remarkably short period of time, members of this club achieved tremendous distance fly casting results.

What is incredible is how Sam Davis was able to accomplish so much in less than a year's time. I think his experience will be helpful in inspiring others to start similar casting clubs. I recently interviewed the 41-year-old angler/caster/scientist. Here are some excerpts, which could serve as a blueprint for forming other casting clubs:

*Q: When did you get interested in casting? How long ago?*

**SD:** I got the tournament casting bug in England during the winter of 2002 after I accompanied a friend to a distance-casting lesson. He wanted to obtain his *55-Yard Club* qualification and was heading to see Iain Thomson (co-founder of the *55-Yard Club*) to get some more pointers. [*Note: To become a member the caster must cast a fly 55 yards or more.*] I listened to Iain and started playing around with the Single-Hand fly distance outfit. Iain said I displayed a natural casting ability and encouraged me to pursue the *55-Yard Club*. I became more and more intrigued with the mechanics and art of tournament casting. I also realized that this sport offered plenty of physical and mental facets for me to pursue without being near a fish. I am also one of the fortunate few to enjoy both fishing and casting with equal zeal. I qualified for the *55-Yard Club* in mid-2003, and I established the British Fly Casting Club (BFCC).

**Q: You've done a remarkable job in promoting casting in England. Did casting exist in Britain in recent years prior to your involvement or was it dormant?**

**SD:** Thanks. The answer is yes to both your questions. Tournament casting has enjoyed a long, rich history in England throughout the last century and had been governed, until the mid-1980s, by the British Casting Association (BCA). However, after the demise of the BCA, tournament casting in any organized fashion became nonexistent, except for some informal accuracy events at a few U.K. game fairs, until the creation of the BFCC in mid-2003. Conversely, tournament surf casting in the U.K., which is managed by the U.K. Surfcasting Federation, has a large following.

**Q: What were the important steps in starting your casting club?**

**SD:** First, I was confident in my ability as a leader, motivator and organizer. Second, I made it a goal to set up a club that offered something constructive and fun for those who wanted to cast as an angler and/or tournament caster without being choked by someone else's established rules, history or politics.

Furthermore, since I was so excited about tournament casting, I just wanted to share my excitement with other fishermen, which would in turn provide me with friends to cast with. So that's the background.

Based on my time in the U.K. tackle industry, I realized immediately that the pool of potential casters for the BFCC would come directly from two groups, one large and one microscopic: The large group, of course, was the angling community and the small one was a leftover clutch of experienced tournament casters from the BCA era. Although, I wanted to open up tournament casting to those who weren't fishermen, I knew it was vital to start with those who could relate to casting as part of their sport first.

So with these two groups in mind, I decided to form an organization that would give something positive to both. For example, free instruction was offered to all casters on tournament days, which should translate into more productive fly fishing. A distance badge system that provides a mental boost to those casters who were searching for a tangible goal-related casting system. For the more competitive types, we offered tournaments to test their nerves, level of physical conditioning and ability to translate practice into performance when it really counted.

After experimenting with these and other things, I began to have a clear understanding of what to offer the casters, so the next step was to pursue those individuals who were not only interested in casting, but who were willing to devote their own particular professional talents to improving the club. For example, Paul Brown is a creative director for a large advertising firm in Manchester [England]. We worked together and created a unique visual identity for the club. We produced original and visually pleasing logos and certificates for the club. Andy Miller and I collaborated on developing our Web site. Andy specializes in IT with British Telecom. Carl Hutchinson, who is in the tackle trade, provided tackle for our tournaments, and Mike Marshall, an engineer, created all sorts of contraptions that have made our events much more enjoyable. The list goes on but you get the idea: It was important to find and blend talented people who also had a keen interest in casting.

**Q: What were the pitfalls?**

**SD:** Two come to mind. One was guilt by association. Sorry for the pun. Some thought that we were a resurrected BCA, which had a very poor reputation resulting in its dissolution in the mid-1980s. I had to argue my case with many of the old fishing/casting guard to prove that the BFCC was independent (in thought and deed) of the BCA. The other pitfall was simply a case of narrow-mindedness displayed by those critics who have not given tournament casting a chance. In the end it becomes a case of mind over matter. I don't mind and they don't matter!

**Q: How did you get members to join and/or become interested in casting?**

**SD:** Cold calling and e-mail harassment—just kidding— seemed to help the cause. I would call and invite potential members to free casting sessions (sometimes long ones) near my home, so they could see for themselves how some casting games or techniques could improve their own level of casting, which again translates into better fishing.

Some casters would drop by because they wanted to achieve a level of skill to gain the coveted *55-Yard Distance Fly Club* badge, which has been in existence since the old BCA days. I would also talk to potential members on the phone as long as it took for them to give casting a try.

Once the club was up and running I would send our members e-mails to showcase their casting achievements and progress. I also publicized our results in national fishing magazines. Many of the early members saw that I was sincere about helping them improve their casting, sometimes at the expense of my own progress, so they helped to spread the word and others began to join us.

**Q: Did you get help from the media? How about tackle shops?**

**SD:** Yes, we did get limited support from old and new media and only one tackle shop, World's End Angling Centre, which has supported us throughout. Owner Graham Dadswell, a superb rod builder, gave me total rod-building support and offered discounts to club members who wanted their tournament rods built as well. National magazines and angling web sites played an important role in keeping the organization in front of the fishing public. Magazines such as *Trout Fisherman* and *Fly Fishing and Fly Tying* would run tournament results and some editorial for free, while Web sites such as *www.sexyloops.com*, *www.fishandfly.co.uk*, *www.ukswff.com*, and *http://home.att.net/~slowsnap/index.htm* have provided either post-tournament briefs, chat room support or both.

**Q: Your club's emphasis is on distance. I believe I read in your Web site that there are future plans to add accuracy fly events. Any plans for this, or do you feel most of the members want to do distance?**

**SD:** I know that the majority of U.K. casters are more interested in distance than accuracy. This thirst for distance over any other casting skill is something promoted to ad nauseam levels by U.K. tackle companies who want to promote their rods/fly lines with advertising slogans like, *"Will put out a full [fly] line."* Since most of our members come from the fly-fishing fraternity who primarily fish purpose-built and heavily stocked trout ponds, lakes, or reservoirs where accuracy skills aren't particularly necessary, the desire to improve accuracy skills is not high on their priority list. I would love to see ACA/ICSF accuracy games become part of the BFCC tournament menu, but at this point in our development, the BFCC needs to offer activities that reflect the interests of its members or potential members, which at this time are primarily distance-based. I personally enjoy accuracy events and I am setting up a course at our inn that will have the full range of accuracy events to entice my clients to give accuracy a try.

**Q: I'm amazed with your group's progress. Some of the distances are incredible. Did these casters have previous distance fly-casting experience?**

**SD:** We have quite a mixed bag of casting experience within the club. Some have never competed in a casting tournament but enjoy casting shooting heads for their distance fishing. Some have done a bit of competitive casting at local and national game fairs and simply wanted to improve their casting performance. Others are primarily interested in the *55-Yard Club.* Then we have a few who are professional casting instructors, either FFF or APGAI, who want to compete and share their skills with the club. And then there is Mike Marshall who was British Casting Champion in decades past but who still harbors the skills and love of tournament casting. And finally, a strong tailwind doesn't hurt either!

**Q: Mike Marshall's Two-Hand Fly Distance casts are incredible!**

SD: At 68 years old, Mike is an inspiration to those elder statesmen and young bucks. He can only handle short bouts of practice or competition, but with his extensive knowledge of loop control coupled with a deep understanding of the process of rod loading/unloading, Mike is able to create the types of casts that sheer brute strength cannot match alone. Log on to *www.thebfcc.co.uk* for details on the club. Mike has contributed heavily to our success.

**Q: Who teaches your group the basics? You did, when you lived in England. Any others?**

**SD:** The BFCC teaches on a free basis only. Instructors on their own time are at liberty to charge their own professional rate. I was quite involved with teaching the basics to all of the beginning casters; however, Mike Marshall has taken over that responsibility since my move to France. Carl Hutchinson, one of our FFF instructors, has also been generous with his time with any member who wanted to improve.

**Q: Do your members fish a fair amount or are they primarily interested in tournament casting?**

**SD:** Without a doubt, most of the BFCC and UKSF casters are fishermen who have been intrigued in various degrees by tournament casting.

**Q: You have many creative aspects to your casting club. Of particular interest are the distance club emblems. I imagine that has been very popular. Right?**

**SD:** Absolutely. From the outset I asked myself what could I offer the casters, which would give them the impetus to improve while celebrating their accomplishments visually to others? Thus the badge (patch) and certificate system were born. In the past the *55-Yard Club* was thought of as elitist since it was viewed as not being related to fishing, but the BFCC have broken down that barrier by creating a system of steps to get to the 55-yard point, and now beyond, with the inclusion of the 65-, 75-, and 85-yard clubs. This way fishermen could gain proficiency in their casts at various distances, and celebrate the moment with a handsome badge.

**Q: What are some of the BFCC's future goals?**

**SD:** This question would be better aimed at Mike Marshall, who has taken over the day-to-day running of the club. However, I would say that increasing club numbers with "participating casters" as opposed to "dues-payers" who never show up is a priority. Also, offering the casters a lively and interesting array of casting events is paramount to the continuing success of the BFCC. I think too much energy goes into worrying about how to get the "general public" excited about viewing a casting tournament. I am more interested in having lots of happy casters who in turn will make future events bigger by increased participation. Except for the ICSF type events, the world is our oyster in terms of what type of casting events we offer; so keeping things fresh is something Mike and I discussed constantly. Finally, finding games that are fun to play and offer some sort of skill growth will ensure that the BFCC remains an important part of U.K. casting.

**Q: You participated in the World Casting Tournament in Switzerland as a USA member. Was this your first world competition? Tell me about your emotions at the tournament?**

**SD:** Yes, indeed, it was my first world competition. Until then I had only competed in two BFCC tournaments as I concentrated primarily on club management up to that point, so the learning curve was steep but fun. My feelings about being at Bern, Switzerland, were strong and positive, but on two very distinct levels. As an American, I was immensely proud to be part of a wonderful and talented team of guys representing a great country. On another level, I was also proud to see the return of the U.K. team to international casting sport after a very long absence. I know that I helped make this happen and was grateful to witness a world record being broken by U.K. team member, Peter Thain, in the 18-gram [plug casting] distance event. The most frustrating time for me at Bern was during Event 2 [Single-Hand Distance Fly], which is normally a very strong event for me. My lack of experience casting on a platform was realized when I found it difficult to cast with a strong right-to-left tailwind. Every time I executed my power stroke the leader would hit the platform, thus deflating the acceleration. The high point for me in the competition wasn't that I beat my personal best in Event 5 [1/4 oz. distance spinning] by over 30 feet with a new rod that I only had 30 minutes of practice with on that day, but that I saw Henry Mittel take the Bronze in Event 8 followed by Steve Rajeff winning the Gold. Tournament casting is indeed a wonderful sport!

# Conversations and Reflections

Interviews with some of the avid and successful tournament fly casters.

~~~~~~~~~~~~~~~

**Zack Willson** (ZW), *one of our all-time great casters, has won numerous awards and honors first as a Junior Division caster, then in the Men's Division and finally in the Senior's Division. His numerous successes have been in both the accuracy and distance competition. He has been selected for the All-American casting team 35 times!*

**Q: Zack, how did you get interested in casting?**

ZW: My introduction to casting came in 1939 at the age of seven when my dad took me to a Columbus [Ohio] Casting Club practice session. I didn't really do any casting that day, but mostly played around the pond. My first actual casting started at the same location at age ten. Dad had fixed up a 5/8 oz. plug-casting accuracy outfit for me. He showed me the basics of a cast and told me to go out on the dock and have fun. If "fun" meant picking out backlashes, my fun was enormous that first day.

**Q: How many years have you been casting and how many Nationals have you attended?**

ZW: In terms of actual casting, it's 63 years. By age twelve, my 5/8 oz. plug-casting game was coming along to where my scores were in the 92 to 96 [out of a possible 100] range.

I've participated in 48 Nationals. My first was in 1946 at Indianapolis, Indiana. My score of 95 came in second in the Junior Division. That first National is still very fresh in my memory and included many "firsts" in my life. First meal at a restaurant (no fast food places in those days). First time out of the state of Ohio. First time to stay in a hotel. First time to see a burlesque show! (Dad said, "Let's not mention that one to mom.")

Another "first" at the tournament was watching Henry Fujita Sr. cast the Dry Fly Event. I had not yet tried fly casting, but dad was getting started in it. One of the main reasons we went to the tournament was to watch Henry cast Dry Fly. When Henry was on deck, Dad came and got me so we could get front row seats. It was something. The wind was blowing so hard that I don't know how Henry stayed on the platform, but he spread his legs a little extra and crouched down to brace himself and proceeded to hit nine targets for a score of 99 [perfect score is 100]. There were more than 100 casters in the event. The next best score was 97.

**Q: What's your favorite fly game?**
ZW: The Dry Fly Accuracy. During one stretch of 20 Nationals I didn't score lower than 98. There were a dozen of second and third places but no win. Guess what? My son Steve won it. He shot a 100! I took a lot teasing from Steve and his cheering section, which included Allyn Ehrhardt and Dick Fujita. I finally won the event six years after Steve did. Rajeff and I cast 99 to tie. We shot 99 again on the cast-off. On the next cast off, Rajeff scored 99 and I cast 100.

**Q: How often do you practice? Do you have a routine for practicing?**
ZW: My practice currently is infrequent, primarily done at tournaments before each event. However, there is a small pond in a city park in Upper Sandusky that I use about once a week in the summer to get the feel of my tackle. There was a time in the 1960s when practice was an everyday thing. In 1965, in preparation for my first World Tournament, I

averaged 30 hours a week of practice for the eight weeks prior to the tournament. Notes were kept on every practice session for every event. So those are my extremes. Then and now.

**Q: You mentioned casting at the World Tournament. How many have you entered, or was that your only one?**

ZW: I have cast in six World Tournaments. Only the one in 1965 was during my very competitive years and was my most successful. My last World Tournament was 21 years ago in Canada.

**Q: Do you fish these days and, if so, what's your favorite species?**

ZW: Fishing the past 25 years has been mostly with my favorite fishing partner, Marcia. We do most of our fishing from our bass boat. Of course, we catch lots of other species in the pursuit of bass. Since my retirement we have spent the last 12 winters at a fish camp on Orange Lake, Florida. We have been going there for the past 25 years, but just for a week or two per year before retirement. Bob Budd, a great tournament caster and fisherman, who fished there a lot in the winters, told us about it 30 years ago. He said it was the best bass fishing in the U.S., so we had to go see for ourselves.

**Q: Is it true that you do not have sight in one eye? I note that you are an extremely accurate caster. How do you do it? I mean, most of us need the depth of field and even then we have problems.**

ZW: Yes, my sight was lost in my right eye 14 years ago. The medical terminology was Central Retinal Vein Occlusion, which the doctors tell me happens to about one person in every 30,000. Unfortunately, it is one of the few eye problems for which there is not a corrective procedure, although the ophthalmologists keep telling me they're working on it. Only having sight in one eye did not effect my distance casting to any great degree since you are not really concerned about stopping a cast. It is, however, quite a problem for accuracy. In fly casting I start each event knowing the targets are approximately 20- to 50-ft. and try to figure out how many strips it takes to get to from one to another and proceed accordingly. There is nothing very scientific about it, just a lot of guesswork. You "feel" your way around the targets and the second time around is always easier than the first because you know the distances better. In plug casting, I changed my delivery in order to keep the plugs a little lower and on a more direct flight to the targets. Actually, accuracy casting the past 14 years has continued to be fun despite my problem and has presented a real interesting challenge. Besides, it gives me a built-in excuse when my scores are bad.

**Q: What is the casting accomplishment that you are most proud of? One plug event and one fly casting event.**

ZW: Winning the World All Accuracy in 1965 with a new world record score would have to rank at the top. That combination, which has since been dropped from the World program, consisted of Skish Fly, Skish Spinning, Skish Bait, and the accuracy part of Combination Fly. Skish accuracy events were very good for me at that time as I already held the ACA Skish All Accuracy record established at the 1963 National. That world record stood for about ten years until a fifth accuracy event was added to the program.

**Q: Do you have a particular strategy in mind in distance fly casting? It seems that you make a cast, and each succeeding cast goes farther and farther.**

ZW: My strategy in distance fly casting has always been to get a good scoring cast down on the first cast by the simplest possible means keeping my line clear of tangles while making the smoothest possible stroke. Once that is done, hopefully on the first cast, my thoughts turn to accomplishing different objectives with each subsequent cast while continuing to increase power until reaching maximum rod speed by the last cast.

**Q: What are your suggestions for making tournament casting more popular?**

ZW: Our sport is much too complicated with way too much equipment involved. We need simplicity. Four events would probably be our best chance. An accuracy plug event (5/8 oz. would be my choice), an accuracy fly event (Dry Fly my choice), a distance plug event (1/4 oz. One-Hand Spinning my choice), a distance fly event (Angler's Fly my choice). All casters would have to use standard, modern over-the-counter tackle. Our current program is fine for those already in the games with tackle, but not good for the new casters. Next we need to get national TV exposure. We need to modify our flies, plugs, and lines so that our events become more spectator friendly. After the right exposure we will need individual casters to take the message to inquiring groups with demonstration of events and distribution of literature on how to develop a casting program and become affiliated with ACA. The family aspect of our sport should be emphasized; we must let people know of the various competitive classes and divisions for young and old, women and men.

# Harvey Beck *(HB) is clearly Canada's foremost caster today. He often competes in B.A.S.S. fishing contests in addition to the casting tournaments.*

**Q: *What advice would you give a person who is interested in becoming a better fly caster?***
HB: Foremost, make practice fun, and to challenge themselves. For example, when practicing alone, suppose you cast 92 in accuracy, try to cast 93 or higher the next time. There aren't many things more boring than false casting to a target over and over. But you can make a game or a challenge out of it. For example: How many targets can you hit in a row? Or how many casts does it take to hit ten targets? Keep a record. Then try to beat your score the next time.

**Q: *That's excellent advice. When, why and how did you get interested in casting?***
HB: I was introduced to casting by my parents, especially by my mother, Audrey. She bought a rod and reel to go fishing with my father. She had problems casting with it and returned it to the store. The sporting goods manager wondered if she was using it correctly. He then suggested she could get

some casting lessons from the Toronto Anglers and Hunters Club (now known as the Toronto Sportsmen's Association). My dad went along. They found it was an excellent family activity and then brought Nancy, my sister, and me along. My parents enjoyed their fishing more, because now Nancy and I were better casters, so our parents didn't have to spend much

of their time untangling our knots and backlashes. Everyone had more fun fishing.

I entered my first tournament at age five. I came in last; things have gotten a little better from then.

**Q: I'll say. You're one of the premier casters. What is your practicing regime these days? Do you practice a lot or just cast in tournaments?**

HB: Unfortunately, I don't have a chance to practice much for tournaments. However, I do a lot of fishing and most casts go where I want them to land, so, in a way, I stay in tune.

**Q: What's your favorite fly event, Harvey?**

HB: The Angler's Fly Distance. It takes much more skill and timing than the brute strength of the other distance fly events. I've seen women and seniors beat a lot of men because they relied on timing. Truly, a humbling experience.

**Q: What's your single best tournament casting accomplishment that you are proud of? National/ICSF?**

HB: I have been the Canadian casting champion many times and won medals at World games and World Casting Championships. Fly events on the whole haven't been too memorable for me. I have never scored 100 in any accuracy event, a few 99s but never a perfect 100. I have drawn blood a few times in some distance events and had a few "road maps" up and down my back from hitting myself on the forward casts, but I've done pretty well.

I was at a Canadian casting tournament a number of years ago. Competition among a few of us was intense. We were casting Salmon Fly [Two-Hand Fly Distance]. The wind was very strong, usually a good thing. But it was so strong nobody could get his back cast to straighten out. I had only made a few casts and found I was having the same problem. I then put all my effort into a back cast, as much as I would have on a final forward cast. The line straightened out behind me. I then launched my forward cast and the line took off and soared. I knew it was a boomer. What a wonderful feeling! I started to reel in. I was told that I still had four minutes to go.

"That's okay! I still have two more events to cast," I answered, wishing to save my energy. My cast measured 272 feet. My longest ever. You don't forget those casts.

**Q: I understand you compete in B.A.S.S. tournaments. I assume this is all with plugs/spinning. What's your proudest moment on the bass circuit?**

HB: I am still very active in B.A.S.S. tournaments. In bass fishing, the "last win" is always the best. My proudest moment was probably the first time I beat Bob Izumi in a tournament. Bob is the Canadian version of Roland Martin. He had done well in tournaments for years and has a popular TV show here in Canada. He was someone I admired and looked up to, and so finally when I beat him it was something special. I feel the same way when I beat Steve Rajeff. It doesn't happen often but if it does, it becomes doubly rewarding.

# Henry Mittel *(HM) is one of our most consistent winning tournament casters. Born in East Germany, Henry came to the United States in 1991 and eventually earned his Ph.D. in physics from the University of Central Florida. He later moved to the San Francisco Bay area where he quickly discovered the Oakland Casting Club ponds. In less than 24*

*hours he was participating in his first casting tournament in the U.S.*

**Q: You've made it to the top among the very elite casters in the U.S. How often to you practice and where do you practice?**

HM: I typically do two or three distance sessions per week. On my commute home from work I stop by a public park, which has several soccer fields. Each session is 1½ to 2 hours (if my lower back allows) and I try to fit two events into each session.

I practice plug accuracy during my lunch hour. There is a grass strip between two parking lots next to my company. I set up a wooden target, and I try to cast every workday when possible. On Saturdays, I practice fly accuracy at the ponds—typically three to four hours (including breaks for coaching, etc.). That's about 12 hours in a normal week plus any time at Sunday tournaments.

**Q: Do you get nervous in competition? If so, how do you control this?**

HM: I get a little nervous—not as much as it used to be. For bigger tournaments, I get nervous anywhere from minutes to weeks before the competition. I think that this nervousness prepares me for the event. During the event, I am typically busy concentrating on the things I should do. If that works, I can do well. Of course, I get nervous if I am getting a really good score and only a couple of shots are left. Breathing deeply helps but the only thing that really does it is to concentrate not on the score but what I need to do to cast well.

**Q: Suppose you have a good game in accuracy going and you miss a target with a "bad" cast. What do you say to yourself or what do you do to recover?**

HM: Minor bad casts can be overcome by either stepping back both physically and mentally to regain composure or by ignoring them and concentrating on the things I need to do. Really bad casts are very difficult to handle. The only thing helping me is the thought of redemption: *Let's at least get the rest done right.*

**Q: Let's say you were on a deserted island and could practice only one event. Which would you choose?**

HM: Well, if I were on that island only for a month or two, I would clearly choose the Two-Hand Spin Distance. If the "engagement" was indefinite, I might choose Salmon Fly Distance [Two-Hand Fly Distance]. Maybe I wouldn't want to risk getting sick of my current favorite!

**Q: What do you think is the single most important factor missing in order to make tournament casting more popular?**

HM: Kids! Kids' programs, hundreds of groups of kids practicing, competing on many levels as individuals and teams. Kids growing up to adulthood who understand tournament casting as both a serious sport and a great recreational activity.

The second most important factor may be that too few of us promote the sport of casting. Let's face it, when it comes to the recreational aspect of casting it's a distant second to virtually all people interested in fishing. Given the choice of spending a few hours trying to catch fish or casting at some fishless pond, we know how many people currently make the choice of going fishing versus going casting. If we give the choice between exciting, nerve-wracking, action-packed tournaments with meaningful winners and going fishing without catching anything, the outcome could still be in favor of going fishing but with a huge increase on the casting side. The question is how can we GIVE people that choice.

**Q: Before a tournament or an event, do you mentally go over some of the strategies for winning or do you just cast?**

HM: Well, obviously the "strategy" for winning is to get the best score possible. For that, you have to hit every target or try to make that perfect distance cast. There is not much to think about other than what it takes to make that happen. Maybe I think about the same things all the time and don't even realize it anymore. But, yes, there are things that are worth going over before you cast.

In distance events, it's good to know the average wind direction and confirm that it's still the same when the clock begins to click. Is the wind steady or should you wait for a gust? Did you check the ground? What about weeds that could tangle the line? In fly distance, it makes sense to have a plan as to how many casts one should try to make. However, that depends mostly on one's skills. I used to try to make as many casts as possible in the hope to get that one that soars. Now, with a bit better technique, I take breathers to regain strength. If I have a good cast already marked, I may even wait for a favorable wind.

In accuracy events, knowing the wind and lighting conditions in advance makes it easier to adjust accordingly. Perhaps choosing the color of a plug or fly could be important.

**Q: Do you use any photographic equipment (video camera, etc.) to check your casting style, particularly in distance events?**

HM: Yes, I own a digital video camera. I bought it specifically to record and study the casting techniques of others. Of course, I eventually took footage of myself and what do you know: some major bad technique issues became glaringly obvious. Unfortunately, it is a lot of work to make a quality video to see more than the obvious. I shouldn't shy away from that effort, though —considering the payoff potential. Nor should anyone else who has access to such equipment.

**Q: Finally, as a top tournament caster, who obviously has his act together, what are the steps you'd advise a beginner or intermediate caster to do in order that he/she may rise to a higher level?**

HM: For the beginner: learn the techniques and practice them! For the intermediate caster: learn the techniques better and practice, practice, practice. Motivation is the key at all ages or stages. If one can find ways to motivate oneself—to learn the techniques and to practice—one will become competitive.

# Edward Lanser *(EL) has been and is a keen casting competitor, starting out as a teenager and now casting and winning his share of casting titles as a Senior. He has won many casting tournaments and holds several records.*

**Q: How and when did you get interested in casting?**

EL: In 1946 my family took me on a trip and we spent some time at Benton Harbor, Michigan. I was 11 at the time. I walked on a pier and was fascinated by people catching yellow perch. One man saw my interest in fishing and said, "Would you like to try this?" I did and caught some perch. I was hooked. I told my father and we bought some tackle, cane poles, and went fishing together. Later, back home, we noticed that there was some casting instruction in the St. Louis area and I went there. It was casting at targets. I found this very interesting and loved the competition and I just kept casting.

**Q: What's your favorite fly event?**

EL: Two events, really. The Dry Fly Event and the Two-Hand Fly Distance. The Dry Fly certainly is a very graceful event and teaches the importance of rhythmic casting, judging distances visually while false casting, presenting the fly accurately but softly to a target.

I love the Two-Hand Fly Distance because again you must do everything exactly right. There isn't much room for error; power alone won't do it. It's a smooth blend of rhythm, timing and power; if you do everything just right, you can launch extremely long casts. Again, timing is essential. The mistake that some newcomers to the Two-Hand Distance Event make is to use too powerful of a rod. I had this problem myself at first until I went to a softer rod and started hitting the long casts. Casts of over 200 feet.

**Q: What advice would you give a person who is interested in becoming a better caster?**

EL: Even more importantly than practice, practice, practice is to find someone who knows what casting is all about and have him coach you. Undoubtedly this is the best way, because in fly casting there are all those little things that enter into the picture. Loops. Rod strokes. Line release. So many things.

I find that it helps to wear a glove on the casting hand. Just about all baseball players wear gloves, because it helps them hold on to the bat better. Same thing applies to casting.

**Q: What is your practicing regime. Do you practice or just cast in tournaments?**

EL: When I first got started, I used to practice several times a week plus enter tournaments. There were three casting clubs in our area in those days so there was plenty of activity. Today I practice before a tournament. I have a place for distance. For accuracy, I put out some targets on a little lake.

**Q: What's your single best tournament casting accomplishment (that you are proud of)?**

EL: Well, several. Casting 100 in Dry Fly at a National is, of course, a thrill. And 267 feet in the Two-Hand Fly Distance. And 180 feet in the One-Hand Fly Distance to set that record for Seniors.

**Q: You've made some tremendous casts in the Two-Hand Fly Distance. What is the secret?**

EL: I think using a lighter rod at first helps most people. If you're strong and young like Steve [Rajeff], Chris [Korich] and others, sure, the heavier stiffer rods are good for extreme distances. When you make an extremely good cast, immediately try to remember what you did and keep repeating that cast as best as you can.

# Randy Olson *(RO) is a young, highly skilled angler/ guide and is a newcomer to tournament casting. He does all the fly events but he is partial to the distance events. Very few people have succeeded in the tournament game as quickly as Randy has.*

**Q: How did you get interested in casting?**

RO: I became interested in tournament casting after

competing in different games at various fly-fishing shows—not the hardcore ACA type events, however. I knew I was a good caster, at least when it came to fishing, anyway. After all, I always caught a lot of fish, so I must know what I am doing! While surfing the Internet, I saw how far Steve Rajeff was casting a shooting head and my jaw dropped. I soon realized I had a lot to learn. I also came across your articles on the *www.flyanglersonline.com* Web site. It gave me some great pointers on how to get started. I thought I would practice the way you suggested, as if I were in competition. The first thing to master was all the rules. After I got that down I got into focused practice.

**Q: Okay, then how did you proceed? What was your next step?**

RO: I always liked a challenge so I joined the Golden Gate Angling and Casting Club in California and signed up for the National Tournament. I contacted Henry Mittel because his scores were excellent, and, he always seemed to be battling with Steve and Chris Korich for top honors. He gave me lots of pointers on casting and was very generous with his knowledge. I purchased all of my distance rods from Dale Lanser of the ACA as well as flies and a couple of books by Cliff Netherton to get a feel for the history of competitive casting. For instance, it was interesting to note that Marvin Hedge was the first to popularize the double haul back in the '30s, I believe. My accuracy rods are rods that I use when fishing—Gatti, Echo and Temple Forks Outfitters.

**Q: What tip would you give a distance fly caster?**

RO: Chris Korich gave me the best advice on grips. I realize any grip is fine as long as the rod moves correctly, but this is my take on how grips affect my casting: While the thumb-on-top grip is fine for accuracy, it is not for distance, at least in my case. Advocates of the thumb-on-top grip say that it is nice for lining up a target (true), and it is the strongest digit to use when applying power to load the rod (also true). The problem is, when you move your arm to the outside when winding up for a long back cast, your thumb rotates around in an ellipse. The rod follows the hand and therefore you end up throwing your line in a circle behind you, thus killing your forward cast. A good forward cast cannot happen without a good back cast!!! Chris got me to use the extended V-Grip. Remember what I said about the thumb being the strongest digit? Well, the bone at the base of your index finger is a much more solid "brace" from which to launch the rod than a thumb that has two joints.

**Q: What kind of fly casting distances in the Two-Hand Fy Distance Event have you attained?**
RO: The very first time I cast the two-hand rod, I cast exactly 150 feet. It was exciting, but to be at the top I knew you would have to almost double that amount! At the end of last year I made a couple of casts of 248 and 247 feet respectively, which I am content with for now. My best competition cast is 205 feet, which is far from where I want to be, but not having "20 years of experience" in tournaments like many competitors, I am probably more nervous than most.

The other thing I learned is how important the trajectory of your cast is. My mistake the first two years was that I was "anchoring" the two-hand rod with my left hand, and casting with my right, which is a common technique in Spey casting. Some other techniques are using the right hand as a fulcrum and casting with your left hand, and a combination of the two. But when going for extreme distances, you need to aim your cast really high and use both hands to cast the rod, not just one. John Seroczynski and Dick Fujita have both hammered me on my trajectory. I was too low but have made good progress.

**Gord Deval** (GD), *through the years, has been one of the most successful Canadian casters. Despite several near-death experiences, this Senior Division caster can still throw a fly more than 200 feet with a two-hand rod.*

**Q: What's your favorite fly event?**

GD: I like most of the games but my favorite is the Two-Hand Fly Distance. It's nice to see that line soaring!

**Q: What advice would you give a person who is interested in becoming a better caster?**

GD: The best advice I can give anyone is to join an ACA casting club, if one is near you.

**Q: When and why did you get interested in casting?**

GD: The book that got me interested in competitive casting was Earl Osten's book (*Tournament Fly and Bait Casting,* A.S. Barnes, 1946).

**Q: What is your practicing regime?**

GD: I enjoy practicing almost as much as competing. Actually, it is the same, but you are competing with yourself. If you cast a fly 160 feet, then you try to cast 165 feet on your next cast. I practice casting as much as I can find time for now. I'm limited, however, by various time-consuming projects I have.

**Q: What's your single best tournament casting accomplishment that you are proud of?**

Beating Steve Rajeff a couple of times to win Gold medals in the ACA Nationals in the Salmon Fly Distance (now called the Two-Hand Fly Distance) and setting a record 249 feet in 1982. The salmon distance event was cast in Lexington, Kentucky. I was casting with three broken ribs and my chest all taped up. I passed out after the fourth or fifth cast. Win (Doc) Burke brought me around with smelling salts and told me that I had won the thing. Anyhow it was the record—one that's permanent because the rod length was changed later. Also I set another record, 173 feet in 1980 in the Angler's Fly that stood for seven years.

**Q: About how many gold medals have you won in Nationals?**

GD: A few dozen.

**Q: Gord, you've written a number of fishing articles and books. Aren't you working on a book now? Also what is your favorite species and method?**

GD: I've had five books published. My latest, *Magical Waters and Memories*, is due for release in 2006.

Another book, *Casting About with Gord Deval,* is sold but not yet published. I've written about a dozen magazine articles. My favorite species is the beautiful brook trout and fly fishing is my method of choice.

**John Seroczynski** *(JS) does it all. He fishes, hunts (mostly with a bow) and is one of our most active tournament casters today. Besides winning his share of tournaments, John is president of the American Casting Association (ACA) and a member of the distinguished Casting Hall of Fame.*

**Q: How did you get interested in tournament casting and how old were you?**
JS: I was 10 years old and was working as a cleanup boy at J. W. Millikan Sports in Hammond, Indiana. Some of the customers decided to start the Hammond Casting Club in Harrison Park across the street from our home. They needed a ring boy to put out the targets three days a week and I became that boy.

**Q: What attracted you to tournament casting?**
JS: I was an avid fisherman and I could see how it could improve my casting and therefore my fishing, and I also loved the competition.

**Q: What type of fishing do you prefer?**
JS: I enjoy all types of freshwater fishing with steelhead and bass probably being my favorite. Someday I'd like to fish for bonefish and tarpon.

**Q: How many years have you been seriously involved in tournament casting?**
JS: I started in 1953…52 years ago! Time flies!

**Q: What's your favorite fly event?**
JS: I prefer the accuracy events, but the distance events are in my blood, too. I really enjoy competing for the All-Round. I

only wish I had the time to be one of the big guns. If I could only cast one event it would be a toss-up between Trout Fly and Dry Fly accuracy events, but I lean to the Trout Fly. In the distance event I'd say that it's the Two-Hand Distance Fly.

**Q: You're among the best of the best casters in North America. How often do you practice and where do you practice?**
JS: I concentrate on the accuracy events in my backyard, and I do that maybe one two-hour session a week. As for distance, I can only throw the Anglers' Distance Fly in my yard.

**Q: Do you get nervous in competition? If so, how do you control this?**
JS: I wouldn't say I never get nervous, but I learned long ago that the nerves can be controlled, and, when I'm in a zone, no distraction will bother me. If I screw up on a cast, my only concern is knowing what I did wrong and then I concentrate on not doing that again. Like everyone, I like to win and I totally love shoot-offs even though I don't always win. They teach and force me to be focused.

**Q: Suppose you have a good game in accuracy going and you miss a target with a bad cast. What do you say to yourself or what do you do to recover?**
JS: I've said the following more that once: "Dummy, don't ever lay down the fly until you're sure." In distance fly, when I think I've waited long enough for the forward haul, I wait a little longer.

**Q: Before an event, do you mentally go over the strategies for winning or do you just cast?**
JS: I sit down and try to get focused, or, as they say, get "in a zone." In the accuracy events (especially in the fly games), I stand in the box before the event and study the target

layout, distance between the targets, the wind direction and velocity, because I may want to change to a heavier line or rod. Light conditions are also important. Do I want a yellow or a white for the fly? How about the color of sunglasses? That's an important thing that some casters ignore. Of course, I make sure that my tackle is ready and hopefully in perfect condition.

**Q: You've had many outstanding casting accomplishments. What do you think are your three most important victories or accomplishments?**

JS: Three things stand out far more than any others:

1) My induction into the ACA Hall of Fame in 2003 was so unexpected I was, for one of the few times in my life, speechless.

2) When I was in an Intermediate Division at a Columbus National, I was the last to cast. When I stepped into the on-deck station, there were already Wet Fly scores of 97, 98 and 99. In those years you chose a fly from the official box of flies. The station captain was Henry Fujita, Sr.—in my book, the master of the fly rod—and he realized that I was very nervous. I couldn't even put that fly on that heavy wet fly leader. Henry, in his wisdom and in an effort to calm my nerves, said, "Let me tie it on, Johnny. Don't worry. This is the last fly in the box and it's a '100'." I still have that fly, that leader and the Gold 100 Club pendant for setting a new National record and my first perfect score at a National. It is my most cherished award over the 51 years.

3) Making the All American Team is also very high on my list because it denotes that you are one of the "best of the best."

**Q: What do you think about cash tournaments? It appears that some nonACA tournaments are going that way.**

JS: We need tackle industry backing, but cash tournaments have proven recently that they bring new interest to the sport.

**Q: What is necessary to make tournament casting a very popular outdoor activity?**

JS: We need the media and in order to get them we need the

tackle industry to be involved like they were for so many years, long ago.

**Q: What are your suggestions to a beginner or intermediate-skilled caster, so that he/she may advance to a higher casting level?**

JS: Don't try to learn all of the events at one time. First, start with the ones you do best. Develop some confidence. This will help you realize how practice can help you improve on what you already know. Second, I think you should find three or four friends or family members who could enjoy casting. It's much more enjoyable doing things with others rather than by yourself. The competition will fuel your drive to improve.

**Q: When one reads Cliff Netherton's two great books** (History of the Sport of Casting: Early Times **and** . . . Golden Years)**, one realizes the close relationship that existed between tackle manufacturers and tournament casters. Today, many tackle companies have little or no knowledge of tournament casting. Is there a way to change this?**

JS: This subject is the most important thing we need to work on and we must do it fast. Today's tackle industry is made up of young people who are not old enough to know how important our sport was and should again be. It's important to our future, but it's also important to the tackle industry's future and growth.

# Dusty & George Revel *(DR) & (GR) were 13 and 14 years old during the 2003 Nationals when I first met them. I was amazed not only with their tremendous casting but also with their knowledge of fishing and that they could carry on a conversation with any adult.*

**Q: Which is your favorite fly-casting event and why?**

DR: My favorite game is Bass Bug, because I enjoy its fast pace.

GR: Mine is the Dry Fly Event. It's really very relaxing, especially now, because I can do it without thinking of all the casting mechanics involved.

**Q: What was your greatest moment in casting competition?**
DR and GR: Still to come. Maybe the next tournament, or the one after that!

**Q: Did you get interested in fishing first and then took up tournament casting later or the other way around?**
DR& GR: We started spin fishing first. Then we started fly fishing. And then became interested in tournament casting mainly to improve ourselves as casters, which, of course, is important in fishing success.

**Q: Do you get nervous in casting tournaments, and if so, how do you calm yourself down?**
DR: I usually do not get nervous before tournaments, but when we first started to cast competitively, I did. To calm myself down, I pretended that I was casting in our backyard rather than in a tournament.

GR: Sometimes, I do get nervous. When I do, I take a couple deep breaths and tune everything out.

**Q: I assume Angler's Fly is your favorite distance fly game. What kind of distances are you getting in practices these days?**
DR: Due to the weather and school, we have not been practicing as much as we should, but I think I would hit about 130 feet pretty regularly.

GR: I am very inconsistent in this event. At times, I can hit 150 feet. At other times I can't break 130.

**Q: What is your opinion of the 5-Weight Distance Fly? How much line do you false cast in this event? Any secrets?**
DR: I love the 5-Weight Distance Fly. I carry about 80-85 feet. I try to use as long a stroke as possible, so I can apply the power more smoothly without causing a tailing loop.

GR: I love it. I can hold about 79 feet and have cast up to 107 feet, but usually about 100. In tournaments? About 90 feet. My secret is long hauls and a shorter stroke.

**Q: How has casting helped your fishing?**
DR: Well, casting has helped my fishing skills immensely. Being

able to put the fly where I want it is one of the most important aspects of fly fishing.

GR: I agree. Casting accuracy is very important in fly fishing. And it makes fishing more fun, too!

# Guy Manning *(GM) The great success of the Revel brothers is due to their dad's encouragement and to Guy Manning's coaching. Here's part of the interview with Guy.*

**Q: How did Dusty and George get interested in tournament casting?**

GM: I would like to say it was all my fault, but it wasn't. Andre, their dad, had (and still has) family living across the street from where Tim and Steve Rajeff grew up in San Francisco. He would tell his boys stories about the Rajeffs' casting accomplishments. About two years ago, Andre and I got involved in a project to put handicapped access fishing docks where the Revels live. Because the boys were always with him I came to know them. They had already obtained a rough foundation in casting from The Fly Shop in Redding, California. They both had 40-foot-plus casts with relatively decent loops. But they lacked an understanding of the relationship between target distance and stroke length and timing. They also needed to work on improving their form, especially the stopping of the back cast.

I offered a lesson and found they were interested in tournament casting. So I bought some 14-inch pizza tins for targets. We worked with the tins for a few months. Then, when the boys expressed an interest in the 2002 Northwestern tournament we bought some PVC irrigation hose and built 24-inch rings. We met every other week and cast for two to three hours. When we got to the Northwestern Tournament, they were amazed at how large the REAL rings [30-inch diameter] were. I had created the smaller rings on purpose.

**Q: Are there other casters who coach them?**

GM: They also met Tony Yap of the San Jose Casting Club.

Tony had spent some time with them prior to my involvement and he still calls them up and meets with them. They get a lot of coaching from other casters, too. George and Dusty also listen to experts at the sports shows and ask many questions. During one distance competition, Dusty was given some advice by one of the tournament directors. This advice was not advantageous to take and he didn't cast as well as he could have.

This actually turned out to be a good thing because it made them both consider that: One, not all advice is good advice. Two, just because it comes from an adult it doesn't mean it's always right. Three, do a little judging of the other person's casting techniques before taking his advice. And, four, it is wiser to stick with what you have already learned and practiced while you are at a tournament. New or different techniques are things to practice after the tournament, when nothing is at stake.

**Q: Does Andre (their father) cast in tournaments?**
GM: Andre makes attempts at it but has never really put in the time to become more than a competent caster. He has taken up the role of scorekeeper and distance/accuracy judge while we are working together. At the tournaments Andre participates as scorekeeper and general helper. I think that the real issue with Andre, as a single father, is his concern for his two sons. We both believe that kids need to find an activity that they can focus their excess energies on. We (all four of us) seem to have accomplished this as a group: The boys have set goals and are pursuing those goals. Andre has helped the boys find and develop an interest in fly fishing. I have taken the boys' raw talent and energies and molded them to the point where Dusty and George can objectively see what skill level they are at. As for fishing, Andre often ends up sacrificing his time to the boys. Andre does most of the rowing when they are on the river.

**Q: What advice would you give adults teaching youngsters?**

GM: It's important with kids to give them some room to do their thing while training. Since the boys both love to do the long double-haul casts, I will usually give them some time just to play at whatever they want during the first part of a session. After a bit, I'll find something they may be doing that will allow me to segue into a lesson mode. We will then practice, and cast for score, using what we just learned. I ask them a lot of questions about techniques and also let them experiment with things they may have considered on their own. I challenge them to think the differences through and tell me why they may feel one thing is better than another.

It is only after all of this that I give my opinion, and why I feel it is better or worse than their approach. Also, I had a few occasions when one of the boys might go into a teenager mode. This is the condition every teenager suffers from when they become convinced that they know it all and that the adult knows nothing. I use two techniques to overcome this. One, since this is usually associated with a demonstration, I will tell them to watch or look at me. Many times I can get their attention back this way. Two, if this fails, I will call them on the attitude. I will say something like, "I'm attempting to show you something important here, but I can see in your eyes that you are not in a receptive frame of mind right now. So I will just stop trying to help you until I see that you are more inclined to listen." It is amazing how quickly they recover when they want to.

**John Field** *(JF) was an outdoor writer on the masthead of* **Canadian Sportfishing** *for three years and a contributor to three other magazines. He was fishing his way across northern Canada when Larry Dahlberg drafted him for four years to do projects for TV, including promotions and editorial. He attended the 2003 ACA National in San Francisco and competed one year later in the 2004 National in Lexington, Kentucky. He won a Bronze Medal (3$^{rd}$ place) in the Angler's Distance Fly with a long cast of 161 feet!*

**Q: How did you personally get interested in tournament fly casting?**

JF: Mac Lord, FFF (Federation of Fly Fishers) Board of Governors, told me I had distance casting potential when I cast a 7-wt. floating line 50 feet past the required 75 feet during the Instructor Certification test. He told me to get a coach and gave me some names.

**Q: What is your favorite fly event?**

JF: Two-Hand Distance. It reminds me of rocketry. I aspire to break the 200-foot mark this season.

**Q: What is your favorite fly fishing species?**

JF: Right now, striped bass.

**Q: You made a quantum leap from the time you visited the San Francisco National in 2003 to becoming a Bronze Medal winner at the 2004 National. Since you live far from a casting club, how did you do it? Lessons? Practice on your own? Using video equipment?**

JF: After videotaping at San Francisco, I studied every distance medalist's casting style, frame by frame. I also had three lessons with Steve and Tim Rajeff. I try to practice every week.

**Q: What do you think is needed to increase the popularity of casting?**

JF: Large prizes to compete with those given at bass events.

# How to run a casting tournament

*Suggestions for fishing clubs, fly shops, fishing lodges & sportsmen's shows.*

## FOR FISHING CLUBS

SUPPOSE YOU BELONG TO A FISHING CLUB and every year it has one or more socials for members and their families. Besides activities for youngsters, raffle and door prizes, you need a zinger!

How about a fly-casting event? Since your group probably is composed of both veteran and novice casters, you could divide contestants into classes (e.g., Class A for those who have had more than three years of fly-casting experience and Class B for those who have less experience). Use Level One or Two (pages 27 and 33) or similar for the novice and Level Seven (page 51) for the more experienced casters. *Tip:* Select events that go by fast and are relatively simple.

While expensive prizes aren't necessary, it's best to offer some sort of an award or prize to casting contest winners. It can be plaques, trophies, club hats, fly boxes, a set of flies, leaders. (Or, here's a novel idea: how about a copy of this book?). You should have several fly outfits available for the casting contest for those who did not bring their own. A 5- or 6-weight outfit is ideal for the accuracy events, and make sure you have sufficient leaders and tippet materials plus practice flies.

Always begin by having an experienced caster demonstrate the event once or twice. If your club has invited family members, encourage the spouses and the older children to try it. Above all, offer encouragement to all casters.

You may want to contact a local fly shop to donate some tackle for prizes. *Tip:* If you receive any merchandise be sure to acknowledge the store's generosity in pre-event promotion and at the start and the end of the casting competitions. Of course, write a personal "thank you" note to the donors.

## FOR FLY SHOPS & TACKLE STORES

A casting tournament is the perfect promotion for your customers and prospects! Good Lord, you won't have to search very far to find balanced fly-fishing outfits! The necessary steps almost suggest themselves:

1.  Do you have an appropriate place to hold a tournament? Unless you have ample room for distance, stick with the accuracy events. Ideally, you will need a cleared area of about 120 x 40 feet, but you could get by with 100 x 30 feet (remember you have to allow sufficient space for a back cast). Perhaps you are located in a mall (what a great place for attracting spectators and potential customers!). Of course, you will need to get permission from mall management and be sure to obtain this well in advance and **in writing**. Maybe there's ample room in front or in back of your store that can be cordoned off. If not, there is probably a park or an athletic field that can be used, but, again, obtain the necessary permission in writing ahead of time.

2.  Regardless of where it is held, make sure the casting area is cordoned off with a high visibility material. A few stanchions and some rope will work provided that you attach some signs at intervals not only to indicate the casting area, but also to promote your event. Use bright colored cardboard and an announcement, such as "ABC Fly Shop Annual Casting Tournament . . . 2 to 4 PM." This will not only warn people of the casting zone for safety but will also publicize the tournament.

3.  Select a date that doesn't conflict with some major event.

4.  Contact the local outdoor writers, local/community newspapers, radio shows and TV stations (remember, fly casting is "in" these days).

5.  Contact some of your favorite tackle suppliers for possible prize donations. Always acknowledge any support in every possible way.

6.  Contact your favorite rod (or line) manufacturers to find out if they have a casting pro willing to provide a demonstration. Some major companies will do this if it appears that it's good publicity for their products.

7.  Use your contact list of clients and prospects. If you have their e-mail addresses, great. You can send them periodic announcements of the tournament, but work well in advance to create a buzz. If you have mailing addresses of customers or prospects who don't have e-mail, send them an announcement through the mail.

8.  Print the rules of the event well in advance of the tournament. You can mail or e-mail these to customers/ prospects, but also place them at various strategic places in your store. Tuck a notice in everyone's purchase.

9.  Before the tournament, rig up several fly rod outfits (including some lighter ones for the youngsters). Prior to the actual competition, have your best caster (you or anyone else) demonstrate the event once or twice. Have

someone with a strong voice explain rules and how the event is cast.

10. Run the tournament. Award the prizes. Important: Take pictures of the winners (and perhaps the youngest or oldest competitors), and send the best ones to your local newspapers with captions.

11. Thank every casting participant and encourage them to enter future events. If you can afford it, give every participant a cap with the name of your store on it. It's good publicity.

12. Thank all the media and tackle companies who helped you.

13. Begin planning next year's event.

I can't think of a better promotion for the relatively small investment than an actual casting tournament. It develops good will, people get to try (and buy!) various outfits, and it's a great way to promote your store's name.

## FOR FISHING CAMPS & LODGES

I always thought that fishing camps/lodges located near water are missing a good bet by not setting out some targets at the dock or other convenient place where guests could practice their casting during nonfishing hours. At many lodges, fishing usually doesn't commence on the day of arrival, so wouldn't casting be a good diversion for the guests?

I spent a lot of time fishing in Canada and even guided one entire summer in my youth. I recall how after dinner guests milled around the dock looking for something to do. On fishing trips to Montana, the Caribbean, South America, Europe—many places—I could see where targets for casting practice or for friendly competition during nonfishing hours could be an interesting attraction.

Most anglers go on one or two major fishing trips a year;

thus, their casting may be a little rusty. This would be an excellent opportunity for them to practice during nonfishing hours. Furthermore, anglers who are not experienced casters could probably use some casting tips from their guides. Makes sense, right?

## FOR SPORTSMEN'S SHOWS

What a great place to hold a casting tournament! Just about everything is in place: A captive, interested audience; tackle manufacturers; tackle dealers; usually an indoor pond; and expert fly casters for demonstrations. It's a natural!

Most of the major outdoor shows usually offer fly-casting demonstrations and instruction and several have presented casting tournaments with mixed results.

What is needed is a fast-paced fly-casting event that is fun, is caster-friendly and has audience appeal. I don't mean to be self-serving, but I believe Level Seven (the "One-Minute" game) is the perfect event for this. Because it takes only one minute per caster, hundreds of casters can easily be accommodated in a few hours. Place a big sports clock, like the "shot clocks" used at basketball games, at a strategic place and you've added an extra dimension and excitement, not only for the competitors but also for the audiences. Add some valuable prizes and some trophies and the casting event's popularity soars.

Most of the sportsmen's shows feature numerous lodges and fishing camps. Perhaps one (or more) would be willing to offer a fishing trip as a grand prize? The possibilities are limited only by one's imagination.

# How to start a casting club

*Casting clubs can be small or large,*
*formal or casual, but they should all have one*
*common ingredient: FUN!*

OKAY, SO NOW YOU'VE PRACTICED the Level-to-Level disciplines and some of the ACA fly-casting events, and you're pleased with your progress. Initially you probably became interested in casting practice because you realized that better fly-casting skills generally result in improved catches. To be able to place a fly a few feet in front of a slurping fish; to be able to cast a longer line than you ever thought possible to reach that wary bonefish; to be able to deliver an air-resistant bass bug or permit fly exactly where you want to place it—well, that's a wonderful payoff and well worth all the practice hours and effort you've invested.

Perhaps one day you conclude that casting itself is fun. "Yeah, I'd rather be fishing, but I can't go all the time. I wish there were a casting club near me …" (assuming you don't live near a casting club).

**Well, start one.**

It doesn't have to be a magnificent shrine like San Francisco's Golden Gate Angling and Casting Club. It can be a casual casting club that is conceived by you and a couple of fishing friends or family members. Here is a checklist to help you:

**THE CASTING FIELD:** First you need to find a convenient casting place, which can be at a park, a swimming pool, an athletic field, a pond or a lake. Water or land. You'll need about 120 feet for accuracy events (remember, you have to allow for a back cast) and maybe 200 feet for distance casting (again, you need room for a back cast), and about 40 feet in width. This should be relatively easy to find. Give some consideration to wind conditions: You want a place that's relatively calm, especially for the accuracy games, and if possible, an area where you can place your targets in different directions to compensate for windy conditions.

**TARGETS:** You don't need anything expensive or complicated, and six Hula Hoops will do for a start; or, you can make your own from an old garden hose (see page 19). Targets should be no problem.

**MEMBERSHIP:** Recruiting other members is usually just a matter of simple "marketing" procedures, and there is no single formula that is applicable to all communities. Here are some avenues for finding other members:

1.  Start with your fishing friends or family.

2.  Contact your local fly shop or tackle store. This can be mutually rewarding. Explain to the owner or manager what you have in mind. List all the advantages to his store. Emphasize that casting will help his tackle sales because better casters catch more fish and logically buy more tackle. Ask him if you can provide an attractive poster and a flyer for his store. Be aware that many fly shops offer fly-casting lessons (for a fee) and this could make an owner hesitant. Explain to him that his new students would benefit from a club where they can increase their casting skills. You might even consider partnering a casting club with a fly shop.

3.  Contact your local newspaper's outdoor writer and tell him about your plans for a casting club and ask for his help. Pick a date (weekend or evening) when you and others will demonstrate one or two events to his interested readers, and, of course, invite the outdoor writer

as an honored guest. If your newspaper doesn't have an outdoor column, send the paper a one-page news release which should include the five *W*s (who, what, where, why, and when) plus your contact phone number and e-mail address. Newspapers are always looking for community projects to write about.

4. Sportsman's or Outdoor Shows: Just about every mid-sized city has an outdoor sport show that generally takes place during the winter months. Some of the shows offer fly-casting exhibitions and instructions by skilled casters. What a great place to get members! Talk to the sport show people. Tell them that you are starting a casting club and ask them if they would place your club's literature or posters at convenient places near the casting demonstrations. Once you have launched a successful casting club, sport shows may even provide a free booth. Obviously you will need appropriate literature and be willing to give casting demonstrations and instructions if requested.

5. Contact other sporting organizations. Is there a fly-fishing club or TU or FFF chapter near you? Or a hunting and fishing club? These are excellent places for obtaining some members, but work in conjunction with these clubs rather than competing with them. *Tip:* Clubs whose memberships are primarily composed of plug casters and spinning enthusiasts may be excellent places for prospecting. Many want to learn to fly cast but may think it's too difficult. Offer to help run a tournament for club members.

6. Other venues for recruiting members will surely suggest themselves depending on your community.

**THE CASTING PROGRAM:** Obviously there is much flexibility to the casting program and much will depend on the membership. You might consider having informal tournaments on some sort of set schedule (e.g., once a week, once a month, whenever). Periodically, you might have a more official fly-casting tournament, with some name like *Season-*

*Opener, Windy-City Fly Casting Championship* or *Waushara County Tournament.*

Keep it simple to start. Select one of the first Level-to-Level disciplines from this book. As your members gain experience and skill, cast the One-Minute Event (Level Seven) because it moves fast and is lots of fun. Try the ACA events after your members have gained fly-casting proficiency. The goal is to present events that challenge the members' skill and ability, but are not so difficult that they become frustrated and look for another activity.

**THE OTHER SEASON:** In the northern climes we associate fly fishing and fly casting as a spring-to-fall happening. The winter? Well, many anglers tie flies or become involved in other activities. But why not offer fly casting?

There may be a high school gymnasium, a health club, an athletic club or some large hall that might be suitable for fly casting during the winter months. You may be able to make an arrangement to use the facilities for a very nominal fee or other value exchange. For fly-casting accuracy events you don't need much room (an indoor basketball court will do nicely), and the fact that dry flies are feathery light means that there would be no damage to the floors (as opposed to plug-casting weights). You will need a few Hula Hoops and make sure that all participants wear the right type of athletic shoes (so as not to damage the floors). You might find that the winter fly-casting sessions and even tournaments become more popular than during the spring and summer seasons be-cause of the plethora of outdoor activities, including fishing.

**ORGANIZING THE CLUB:** After a few sessions and in-formal get-togethers, you should plan a club organizational meeting, inviting all members and prospects to participate. Decide on the appropriate time to have such a meeting (make sure that it doesn't conflict with the World Series, Super Bowl, Air Shows, etc.). Prepare a meeting agenda well in advance; don't play it by ear. Here are some salient points to be included in your agenda and some general statements:

- *Mission of the club:* Agree on the club's mission or vision. For example: to promote fly casting, increase one's skill, develop comradeship, provide friendly competition for those who want it, and, later, perhaps even offer club fishing trips.

- *Casting club name:* Select a temporary name for your club. It can be named after your town, e.g., *Peoria Fly Casters,* or an individual, e.g., *Jimmy Green Fly Casters* (Jimmy passed away recently and was one of the great innovative forces in casting and fishing). Explain that this is a temporary club name and ask for other suggestions.

- *Budget and membership dues:* Develop a budget based on expected costs associated with a modest new venture. How about $20 a year for individual membership or $30 for families? Explain that the money would be used for printing brochures, buying more targets, etc.

- *Election of officers:* Since you and some of your friends initiated the club, volunteer to serve as officers for the first year; thereafter, officers would be elected by the membership.

- *Committees:* If you develop a sufficient membership, you should ask for volunteers for various committees. Examples: *Public Relations* (someone who would contact the media for future publicity of tournaments or practices); *Membership* (someone who would lead membership drives and explore new ways to get members); *Prizes and Awards* (to work with local business for various prizes and donations. Incidentally, prizes don't have to be fishing related, e.g., a gift certificate from a book store or a clothing store, free car washes, dinner for two at a restaurant, etc.). *Club Identification:* Besides a club name, eventually you may want to have a club logo, stationery (to write to tackle companies, park districts, etc.), club T-shirts, caps, etc.

- *ACA affiliation:* You may also want to become an affiliated American Casting Association member club (ACA annual club membership is only $50 per year).

Okay, you and your club are growing and growing. You can offer club fishing trips (local or distant), a picnic/tournament with family members participating, perhaps chevrons for casting accomplishments. Many things.

On the other hand, maybe your club has only a half-dozen members and you want to keep it simple and casual. No problem. I believe the Seattle Casting Club has only three members: Bill Van Natter, his wife Peg and Charles Judy. They've won many medals at National tournaments.

At the minimum, members enjoy a wholesome activity and become better casters because of competition and because they learn from each other.

Casting clubs can be small or large, casual or formal, but they should all possess the main ingredient—FUN.

# Casting: A family affair

HERE IS ONE OF THE MOST INCREDIBLE statistics in competitive activities: **50.2 percent of the casters in the last four Nationals were family related** (parents and children, couples or siblings). I don't know of any other sport or competition that approaches this percentage.

Casting is truly a family affair!

It's usually the parents who encourage their sons and daughters, but sometimes it's reversed. The Gillibert family is an excellent example. Alice Gillibert has been casting for years. During the 2004 ACA National Casting Tournament she cast a fly 150 feet in the Angler's Distance Event, easily topping her previous Women's record of 137 feet, and only 15 feet shy of the Senior Men's record. Very few men, regardless of age, strength, skill and casting knowledge can cast half of a football field like Alice did. My guess is that less than 100 men in North America could cast that far in this event.

Did Alice get interested in casting through Ralph, her husband? "No, Ralph has no interest in casting, although occasionally he'll keep score for us and supports tournament casting. I was introduced to casting through Rene, my son. He was getting interested in fly fishing and going to the casting ponds. His friends Chris [Korich], Keith [Pryor], Steve and Tim [Rajeff] interested him in the tournaments. Then Nicole, my daughter, became involved in competitive casting. At a Golden Gate Casting and Angling Club fund-raiser, Steve Rajeff donated a fly rod, which I won. That was back in 1984. I started going to the casting ponds and getting help from the 'guys.' That year, the National was at Long Beach, California, and Rene and Chris talked me into signing up for the Dry Fly Accuracy Event. This got me started. In 1987 I competed in the National tournament at Portland. I participated in only the accuracy events." Later Alice added the plug and fly distance games to her repertoire.

Besides setting the Women's record in the Angler's Fly Distance at the 2004 National, Alice won three additional gold medals in the three accuracy fly events.

Alice is a homemaker as well as an artist whose business is custom tile and decorative painting. She recently served as ACA president. When does she have time to practice?

"I practice some throughout the year and then before the National I will practice more extensively. The toughest practice is the six inches between the ears. So much of casting is mental. Throughout my casting, there have been many people at the club who have been an inspiration and a help. Chris Korich has always been there with a push and a hooray."

Rene, her son, is one of North America's finest fly casters. He cast a fly an incredible 190 feet, tying Steve Rajeff's ACA record in the Angler's Fly Distance Event at the 2002 National. He also cast a perfect score in the Dry Fly Event at a National and has won numerous medals at Nationals and regional tournaments.

Daughter Nicole has won her share of gold, and sometimes mother and daughter tie in major tournaments, which requires a shoot off. They both try to win, of course, and it's very interesting to watch daughter and mother compete against each other in casting events.

"We both have the competitive spirit," explains Alice, "but we are happy no matter which one of us wins, especially if it is with a good score. ACA has had many family members competing. That's what makes this sport so very special. It's ideal for families whether they want to compete in tournaments or merely practice their casting for the sheer pleasure it provides."

Andy Statt, of Cincinnati, Ohio, and his entire family are avid casters. Beth, his wife, is a superb plug caster, but recently has taken up fly casting and competes in the Women's Division in all three accuracy fly events. Their son, Doug, is a fine fly caster and also competes in the three accuracy fly events. Another son, Tony, has also won a medal in a National. Becky, their young daughter, currently casts only in the plug games, but eventually she will cast the fly games. Andy is an all-round caster and is always up there with the best. He cast a fly 238 feet in the two-hand fly distance in a National.

Billy Peters is another superb caster now competing in the Senior's Men's Division. His daughter, Pam, became interested in casting, and she competes in both distance and accuracy events and has been a member of the U.S. Casting Team at world casting tournaments.

Of course, the famous Rajeff brothers are known world wide because of their incredible casting (and fishing) skills.

The Seroczynski brothers (Phil, John, Jim and Tom) are all excellent casters and they love to fish. All four competed in the 2002 Nationals in Chicago.

Bob Zens, a veteran caster, has competed in the distance and accuracy events since the 1940s. His son Martin is a very able fly caster/angler and has done very well in major tournaments, often scoring in the mid-90s, and sometimes higher in the fly accuracy events. Daughter Julie also casts on occasion. While he is physically challenged, because of a bad hip, Bob still competes in accuracy and sometimes distance events, while sitting down. A few years ago, he tried the Two-Hand Fly Distance and cast 170 feet—sitting down!

Zack Willson and his son Steve have both cast a perfect score (100) in National competition. Zack Sr. was also a competitive casting winner.

The Fujita family is among the most famous. Many felt that Henry Fujita Sr. was one of the three finest dry fly casters in tournament history. Sons Henry and Dick (both casting in the Senior Division) still win in various events.

Ed Lanser has most of his family casting. "In some ways, maybe tournament casting people have been wrong in trying to get youngsters into the games in order to make sure the sport has fresh blood. I think the best approach is to get their fathers or parents interested and they will get their children interested."

*Casting is truly a family affair.*

# Casting for everyone

CASTING IS AN ACTIVITY that can be enjoyed by men and women regardless of age or physical limitations. It is truly a universal recreation that fulfills many parameters.

**CAST AT ANY AGE.** One can be a preteen or in his/her 90s and participate in casting for the pleasurable event that it is. Some are attracted to it for the highs that one can derive from competition while others simply cast for the fun of it. At the young side of the ledger, many youngsters start casting before they are 10 years old, usually with a spinning or casting rod. The CastingKids program, for example, has attracted close to a million kids in two age groups: 7 to 10 and 11 to 14.

Dusty and George Revel, the teenage brothers, are turning some heads as they compete in Nationals. They even cast in the men's division at some major tournaments for added competition. Andre Revel, their father, is delighted that his sons are interested in competitive casting. Says Andre: "Casting has been a great asset in raising my boys. Being a single parent I needed to have them focus on an activity that's positive and healthy. We just happen to find fly fishing something we all enjoy and they excelled at it. Fly casting keeps them busy and teaches them discipline. It has allowed us to meet a very diverse group of people that I find very nurturing for they have been very generous in sharing their knowledge. It has been a great experience for both my boys and me."

George Karsant, another excellent West Coast teenage caster has won his share of medals. His parents do not cast but have taken George to Nationals and major tournaments across the country.

In the Midwest, Andy Tulgetske is a superb fly caster and so are Glen Carl and his cousin Josh Carl. Their parents have taken the boys to many tournaments and fishing trips.

On the senior side, one can only marvel at the casting prowess of Dick Fujita, Ed Lanser, Zack Willson and others as they fling a fly easily over 200 feet with a two-hand fly rod. Despite creaking bones, physical ailments and other aggravations that usually become more prevalent to those over 60, these casters successfully compete in such strength-demanding events as the distance fly as well as nerve-testing accuracy fly games where total concentration and perfect timing are essential.

"Cajun" Bill Clements is casting better now than ever. Although he casts in the Senior Division his accuracy scores are among the best regardless of age. He credits recent eye surgery for this success. "Now I can see!"

Ageless Bobby Spear has been competing in tournaments for many years. He, too, is casting better than ever.

**WOMEN IN CASTING.** Ladies have long excelled in fly casting and are becoming even more involved today. Perhaps no other woman did more for fly casting (and fly fishing) than Joan Wulff, who has not only competed in many Nationals but has also written several definitive books on fly casting and has been featured in instructive videos and films. Although primarily involved in accuracy fly casting, Joan can also throw a long line. In 1960, she made an incredible 161-foot cast to win the distance fly event. She cast in the men's division, since there wasn't a women's. She has not competed for years, but her *Wulff School of Fly Fishing* is one of the best in the country. Joan and her staff have taught many people how to cast. Even gifted tournament casters have enrolled in her school to improve their casting.

Some of the outstanding scores by women at Nationals include: Nicole Gillibert-Kozicki and Mel Gavin shooting 99 in the Dry Fly Event; Brenda M. Banks, casting a 97 in the Trout Fly Accuracy. Cecilia Ray's 97 in the challenging Bass-Bug Event; and Alice Gillibert's 150-foot cast in the Angler's Distance Fly.

In the International Casting Sport Federation (a world-wide casting organization) many women have excelled in casting. Perhaps the most incredible achievement was turned in by Jana Maisel of Germany. Her amazing all-round casting performance should be considered as one of the most outstanding accomplishments in any sport in many decades.

She cast perfect scores (100) in three events—fly accuracy, spinning and 5/8 oz. plug casting—and a fantastic 96 in what is known as the Arenberg Event in which the caster must make underhand, sidearm, backhand and other intricate spinning casts. Her total score for the four accuracy events was 396 out of a possible 400. ***Whoa!***

Let's put this in the proper perspective: She beat the men's highest total score (381) for the four accuracy events by 15 points! And the men's division included the best casters in the world.

But while some women love the challenges of competitive casting, many enjoy it for what it is—a relaxing activity in which problems and stress seem to evaporate in the rhythmic flow of the fly cast. Perhaps there is no greater example than Casting For Recovery (CFR). This is a national non-profit support and educational program for women who have or have had breast cancer.

CFR provides an opportunity for women whose lives have been profoundly affected by the disease to gather in a beautiful, natural setting and learn fly fishing, "a sport for life."

The weekend retreats incorporate counseling, educational services and the sport of fly-fishing to promote mental and physical healing.

Founded in 1996, Casting for Recovery has been offering free retreats across the country. It relies on local volunteers and organizations to support various community-based retreats. Participants are taught the basics in fly casting, entomology, knot tying, fishing basics and, of course, they spend time on the water practicing their lessons via catch-and-release fishing.

Casting for Recovery provides weekend retreats at no cost to the participants including lodging, meals and professional instruction.

Any woman who has experienced breast cancer and has medical clearance from her physician is eligible to attend a retreat. For more information, go to *www.castingforrecovery.org* or call 1-888-553-3500.

Other similar programs are being developed, including Reeling and Healing, which also offers fly casting and fishing. Cathy Sero, a fine angler and winning tournament caster, is one of its instructors. The Web site for this one is *www.reelingandhealing.org.*

**PHYSICALLY CHALLENGED.** Men and women have found casting a stress-reducing, wholesome activity. For example, although several casters have lost sight in one eye, they consistently win in accuracy events on the National level.

A few men use crutches, while others must sit while casting. One of the best accuracy fly casters was the victim of involuntary facial twitching and other neurological problems. His father brought him to a casting club because someone suggested that this activity might help. The young man became interested in fly casting and won several Nationals. He developed confidence through casting and eventually the twitching and nervous contortions virtually disappeared. He went to the university, raised a family and was very successful in his vocation.

Many have succeeded in casting competition despite a variety of physical challenges.

***Truly, casting is for everyone.***

# Confessions of an addicted long distance fly caster

*by Jim C. Chapralis*

IT'S A HOT, SWELTERING, HUMID DAY. Sweat rolls down my face, first in tiny beads, but soon they merge to form an unending procession of rivulets. I walk to the athletic field, which is exactly 192 steps from my front door. I'm relieved that no one is there—kids won't practice baseball in this hot weather—so I have the whole place to myself.

I rig my tackle by the baseball bench and then walk another 153 feet parallel to the fire hydrant. I test the wind by throwing pieces of parched grass in the air, but there isn't even the slightest breeze to fan this northern Chicago suburb. The grass falls straight down.

I stretch the mono shooting line and rub out the kinks from the leader. I then perform a few stretching exercises, twirl my arms around, first clockwise, then counter-clockwise, then swing them back and forth.

"It's important to stretch before any physical activity, especially if it's violent exercise," my physical therapist recommended when he treated my casting arm following a recent fall. Distance fly casting can be violent! So I do my stretching exercises first.

I start with short casts and then lengthen them a few feet

at a time. I question my sanity: Why am I out here in the blazing midday sun? If I had any sense at all, I'd be in my air-conditioned home, sipping some Kool-Aid, laughing at a Seinfeld rerun or the Chicago Cubs or some other comedy.

The 2004 National Tournament is in Lexington, Kentucky. In a way, it's probably good that I'm practicing in this torrid, muggy weather, for it will prepare me for the furnace that blows full blast in Lexington during early August.

My first attempt at some distance is about 120 feet. I try again. The line unfolds back and forth in undulating loops, and when I think I have a good back cast, I put more power into the forward cast and speed up my final haul. The line sails and it looks like it's going to be a fine cast: good acceleration, nice trajectory and a narrow, driving loop. But suddenly the front end of the fly line hits an invisible wall and limps down to earth in a gob of fly line followed by about 10 feet of fluttering leader. This clump lands about a dozen feet from the bench, which makes it about a 140-ft. cast. Sure, if it had straightened out, it would have been 165, maybe more. But it didn't. It almost never straightens out on this practice field. Something about down drafts. *Bummer!*

I've got a couple of weeks' practice time prior to the tournament. By now I'm soaking wet from perspiration.

An inner voice speaks to me and I listen: "Jim, let's wind this up. It's too hot and muggy. Why don't we go back to the air-conditioned house, get an ice cold drink, and give this a try on another cooler day! Now wouldn't that be better?"

Yeah, it would. Sounds good. The voice that looks out for my comfort is right. Good advice. This is stupid. I start to reel in, when another voice pops up in my head: "Hold it right there, Jimbo! What are you doin'? Surely you're not quitting! You haven't broken 140 feet and don't give me any excuses about the heat. Remember, 'no pain, no gain'?"

So I strip out some line and vow to continue my practice session and prepare for another cast.

The first voice comes back. "Listen to me, Jim. You're 72. You just had a stent inserted a few months ago because of blockage. In fact, if it weren't for Drs. Sabbia and Kogan, you'd be history by now. You want to make Sally a widow?" The "voice of comfort" definitely had a point. I'm lucky to be alive.

"Jim, Jim, Jim. Don't listen to that quitter!" The "voice of conscience" was back. "I'll tell you what: You hit the bench and you can go in. That's 153 feet. And you know this is a terrible place to cast, because of down drafts, so that means anywhere else that cast would be 163 feet or better. Go ahead now and do a Rajeff imitation . . . or a Korich, or a Mittel. Hit the bench and we go in."

And so I try to imitate the Steve Rajeff style. Then a Korich. Then a Mittel. And I throw in a Gillibert imitation for good measure. All these young West Coasters have collected many gold medals. Rajeff's signature is that explosive delivery on his final cast. Korich, a southpaw, has that very graceful haul—you can draw a straight line from his left casting hand down to his extended right-hand haul on that final cast. Gillibert is not a big fellow but he knows how to develop line

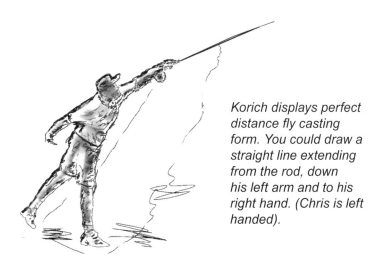

Korich displays perfect distance fly casting form. You could draw a straight line extending from the rod, down his left arm and to his right hand. (Chris is left handed).

speed like few others, and Mittel has become very serious about distance fly now and, heck, he is a physicist so he knows all that stuff about loop sizes, air resistance, gravity and trajectory.

So I do all the imitations. I throw in a few options of my own. I experiment with a longer overhang. I stop the rod higher, but sometimes I strive for a low trajectory. By now I'm exhausted, soaking with perspiration, talking to myself, or, worse, I'm threatening my tackle: "Listen! You better land a lot further if you know what's good for you." Maybe the sun has gotten to me. Good thing no one's around to hear this.

I put everything behind the next cast. And it goes. The leader drapes over the bench so the fly ends up a few feet beyond it. It was a cast of 155 maybe 158 feet. Had it all straightened out it would have been 175 feet . . . maybe more.

So I reel in and drag myself home. Sally tells me I look like a soakin' wet koala bear: "Put your clothes in the hamper and yourself in the shower. Drink some water."

Life is good!


I'VE BECOME active in tournament casting again after a hiatus of about 50 years. Back then, in the "olden days," the rules and equipment were very different. This was before graphite rods were invented. To make a decent distance fly line then, we bought silk fly lines by the foot in various diameters and then we painstakingly spliced about eight different sections together. Nylon fly lines and fiberglass rods were just making an appearance then.

In today's world of graphite rods and high-density tapered lines, the great, young casters talk about loops and rod arcs and paths and trajectory and strokes. So many things. In the late 1940s, Clare Bryan, my casting mentor, usually would say, "Watch this," and he would demonstrate a double haul cast: "Okay, now you do it." And I did, or tried to.

"No, no —like this!" Clare would insist, sometimes impatiently. And I tried and tried some more, and since my desire was genuine, I eventually got the hang of it and some casts soared. The soft, almost parabolic split-bamboo rods we used in those days featured a slower action, which required a different, longer stroke.

Today, aspiring distance fly casters have it easy because they can view DVDs and tapes of some of our best casters. There are excellent casting instruction books and wonderful Web sites that include animated visual graphics of the double haul. Certified casting instructors are available at a fair rate.

Yeah, I cast the other events in tournaments—Dry Fly, and Trout Fly and Bass Bug and some of the plug events—but it's the distance fly events that attract me to the National.

It's an addiction. I daydream of landing cagey big browns at my favorite streams, but I also dream of making that once-in-a-lifetime long cast in a National. My lofty goals may never be fulfilled, but I'm going to try until I can't cast or fish anymore.

I explain my long distance fly casting addiction to John "Coach" Seroczynski, president of the American Casting Association. "Coach, the distance fly games are the main events. The accuracy and all the other events are really warm-up and cool-down events. You know, when Frank Sinatra would perform in Vegas, they would have a couple of acts just to warm up the crowd. Right? Same here. And all games after are held simply to 'cool down' the participants and spectators from the high voltage frenzy of the distance fly games. I mean you don't want them to drive home all 'wired up,' do you?"

Coach laughs. He understands. I think.


MY PRACTICE SESSIONS at the athletic field are not without some humor. Neighbors ask me, "How's fishing?" Or, "Did you catch any today?"

"Naw, but I think I hooked and lost a big one," I answer every time in a serious tone. They laugh. *Ha! Ha!*

One of these days, I'm going to buy several rainbow trout from the fish market and put them on ice in a cooler and take it to my practice field. When the same people ask the same questions, I'll reply:

"Yeah, I caught three beauties this morning. They were hittin' pretty good on a Royal Wulff. Here, take a look."

On second thought maybe I won't do that. With the escalating price of fish these days, I might find lots of fishermen casting for fish on my practice field.

I ALWAYS had a mania for distance, whether it was hitting a baseball or punting a football. Amazingly I remember my longest hit in baseball and a booming punt that I made some 50 years ago. It's no different in distance fly casting. You remember the long ones whether it's in practice or in a tournament. Of course, I remember my longest cast in practice at the athletic field near my house. Let me tell you about it.

It soared, high and mightily, pulling yards of mono shooting line at an incredible speed until there was no more loose line left on the ground. Then I heard that beautiful sound—the screeching reel—which meant that the cast had sufficient energy to angrily demand more line from the reel. I could not see where the fly landed, but I was sure the line had straightened out reasonably well, which is usually the case when you hear the reel scream. I pumped a clenched fist high in the air, in the best Tiger Woods tradition.

"What a cast!" I shouted with uncontrolled exuberance. And then I pumped my fist again. "Bring on Rajeff! Bring on Korich!"

I hurried toward the fly. My plan was to mark the exact spot where the fly landed, then go home, get my 200-foot tape and measure the cast exactly to the inch. Stepping it off is not an accurate method of measurement.

In my excitement and celebratory fist pumping, I didn't notice that the monofilament shooting line had wrapped around my shoe, until it was too late. As I joyously trudged toward the fly, I was pulling in yards and yards of line through the rod, which I had placed on the grass to mark my exact casting position. There was no way I could measure that cast now. Surely it was the longest I had ever made. Was the cast 180 feet? 190 feet? More than 200 feet? I was quite sure it was well over 180, but was it over the magical 200 feet, the benchmark of long distance casters? I'll never know.

THE NATIONALS are only about ten days away. I'm seriously thinking about canceling my trip to Lexington, because I feel lousy. Physically and mentally. I was sure that this was due to all the prescribed medicines I was taking to keep my blood thin following the stent surgery. When I walk up 12 steps in our house, I am exhausted. Before the stent? No problem!

But there was another reason I had lost interest in going to the National. Bus Duhamel was very ill. He is a dear friend of almost 40 years and while he is 93 years old, it was only a few years ago that we waded a Wisconsin trout stream late at night and fooled some big trout. We did this in total darkness: no moon above to guide us through this river section that was booby trapped with a few sunken branches, some rocks, and, of course, several deep holes, too. He was what, 88 or 89 at the time? It was that year, or maybe the year before, that he captured the *Angler of the Year* award for our trout camp because of the incredible catch he made one evening.

Bus was very weak now. I told him I would not go to the tournament. "You go!" He instructed sternly. "And I don't want to hear of a Silver or a Bronze medal. You go and get the Gold. Promise me."

"I promise, Bus. I will win the Gold." But I only said that because he insisted on it. And Bus could be stubborn.

And so I went to Lexington. I felt punk. Not only was I feeling sick, but also my arm now was hurting from that previous fall. I could hardly move it. I had to use my left arm to drink coffee that morning.

It was hot on the distance fields. The excitement was there. The joy on faces. The high anxiety as casters made their final practice shots. Some were making minor adjustments to leader lengths; others sought a little time to themselves to review their strategy. Judges with timers were ready. So were the young fellows out in the field who were trained to mark casts quickly.

I approached John Seroczynski, a superb veteran caster. "Coach, I don't think I can cast. I feel lousy. Can't move my arm much. I feel sick."

"Listen, Jim. You feel good. This is the National. Everyone feels good at the National even if they don't! Now here are my keys, go into my car, turn on the engine and air conditioner and take a nap. You are the last caster and I'll call you."

So I followed Coach's instructions. I fell asleep. The cool air-conditioner and the purring sound of the engine proved to be very soporific.

"All right, Chapralis, you're up next. Get ready," Coach barked.

My rod had already been checked to meet the regulations for the One-Hand Fly Distance Event.

John Seroczynski starts giving me instructions. I felt like a boxer in the ring, getting last minute advice from the manager. "Okay, now take it easy. Wait for a breeze. Stop the rod high. And pull your left arm all the way back on the final haul."

In the One-Hand Fly Distance Event you are allowed a ghillie who can offer advice, strip in the line after a cast for you, and, in general, help the caster. Coach was my ghillie.

I think someone said that Zack Willson was the leading caster in the Senior Division with a 160+ ft. cast. *Yikes!* I tried to find out. "Don't worry about the other scores. You just cast!" Coach said.

I made some fair casts—I think—but I had no idea how far they went. In this event, a participant has five minutes to make as many casts as he wants, and the longest cast determines the winner. The second longest cast is recorded in case of ties. Minutes ticked by. Funny how fast five minutes goes when you are in the caster's box.

"You're doing okay. But wait for a breeze," Coach instructed.

"How far do you think I'm casting?"

"Hey, Chapralis you have enough time for one cast, maybe two. Just wait. There should be another puff of wind in a few seconds."

But I didn't wait. A couple of false casts and then I released my presentation cast. Coach was striping in the line fast, spiderlike, to see if I could get in another cast—a good breeze came up. "Why didn't you wait?" Coach shook his head, but he was smiling, too. "Geez, you should have waited for that breeze."

"Time's up!" Too late. The judge shouted as I prepared to get in another cast.

My two long casts were recorded. One of the boys brought in the scorecards.

"172 feet! You won, Chapralis! You won the Senior Division." Coach announced after studying the card. "Congratulations! If you had listened to me on that last cast and waited a just few seconds for that nice breeze, you might have tied or beaten the Senior's record of 180 feet." I was nine feet short of a new record for seniors.

I was overwhelmed with emotion. A few minutes ago I felt sick. I could hardly move my arm. I didn't think I could cast. Adrenaline does remarkable things. Tears of joy dripped down my face. I was crying and I didn't care.

"Are you okay? Are you okay?" Coach was concerned. I had told him that I had some medical information in my wallet in case something happened.

"I'm fine. I'm delighted to have won the Gold, but I'm mostly happy that I kept my promise to Bus."

The Angler's Distance Fly Event took place right after that. It's a similar event except that casters are restricted to a lighter line (equivalent to a No. 10/11). I also won the Gold for seniors in that event with a cast of 153 feet.

I called Bus. He was in an oxygen tent. He could not speak on the phone. I talked to Mildred, his wife. "Bus is not doing very well," she informed me.

"Could you do me a favor? Could you tell him I won the Gold in distance fly for him?" "Absolutely." I could hear her telling him. Then a little later, she said: "Bus gave a 'thumbs up' sign. And he smiled. He said something but I couldn't understand him. But he smiled."

Bus died a few days later.

I had planned to put the Gold medal in Bus's casket. But

his instructions were that he would be cremated. He didn't want any special ceremony. No hoopla. No speeches. He just wanted to be cremated and for his family to dispose of his ashes. Quiet like.

Bus was that kind of a guy.


IT'S A HOT, SWELTERING, HUMID DAY. Sweat rolls down my face, first in tiny beads, but soon they merge to form an unending procession of rivulets. I walk to the athletic field, which is exactly 192 steps from my front door. I rig my tackle by the baseball bench and then walk another 153 feet parallel to the fire hydrant.

Just like I've done so many times before.

I listen to the two inner voices argue. I make my casts. I need to go farther. The 2005 National Tournament at Dundee, Michigan, is only a few weeks away.

**And I need to practice.**

# Afterthoughts

▶ I'M SURE SOME PEOPLE will purchase this book and expect to find instructions on how to make the basic casts. *Master Your Fly Casting!...And Have Fun Doing It* assumes that the reader knows the basic fly-casting strokes. If you don't know them, no problem. Put this book aside for the time being, and obtain a how-to-fly-cast book. Or view a fly-casting video. Try your public library (some major public libraries have casting videos and books). If you have a computer, you'll find a number of excellent fly-casting Web sites that visually demonstrate the standard casts. Perhaps you know an experienced fly caster who can give you some pointers? By all means enlist his help.

▶ I'VE MENTIONED THE "DOUBLE HAUL" casting technique often in this book. It is essential not only for distance, but also for casting big flies in windy conditions. The best way to learn the basic double haul is to find someone who knows it well to instruct you. Perhaps there is a fly-casting school in your area that teaches the double haul in addition to basic fly casting. Many fly shops offer casting courses. If there is no one in your area, obtain a videotape and study it carefully. Videos by Mel Krieger, Joan Wulff, Lefty Kreh and others are excellent. Once you learn the basics of the double haul, it's just a matter of practice and adjusting.

▶ YOU'LL NOTICE THAT all the accuracy disciplines or events in this book involve casting at targets. Initially, you may want to practice without targets, but after you've honed your basic stroke, cast at targets. Two reasons: Accuracy is extremely important in successful fly fishing and casting on a lawn without targets quickly leads to boredom. Targets offer a necessary challenge. That's true with other similar activities. A novice archer may shoot some arrows to get the feel of the bow, but once he has it, he needs to shoot at a target or he'll quickly lose interest. Can you imagine bowling without pins? Or shooting a basketball without a hoop? The same principle applies to casting.

▶ HERE'S A WAY TO SHARPEN YOUR ACCURACY. After you develop casting proficiency, decrease the size of the target. Instead of casting at a Hula Hoop or a 30-inch target, cast to a smaller target, such as an aluminum pie pan. I don't know why it is, but casters come closer to smaller targets than hitting the bigger ones. Many successful competitive casters know this and pinpoint a spot in the center of the target rather than aiming at the target itself. Guy Manning used 14-inch pizza tins for targets to train the young Revel brothers to be excellent accurate casters (See "Conversations and Reflections" chapter).

▶ IF YOU ARE A FLY TIER tie plenty of practice flies in your spare time. The standard dry fly used in tournaments is easy to duplicate. A few strands of yellow fibers for the tail, a red silk body and a yellow hackle on a straight eye No. 10

*Samples of dry fly, popper and distance fly.*

or 12 hook will do it. You want to tie a similar but smaller fly (No. 12 or 14 hook) for the Trout Fly Event. For the distance events, tie the flies in wet-fly style on a No. 12 hook. For the Bass Bug Event, yellow or white poppers are used depending on light conditions. They have cork bodies and you can use deer hair for the tail. Of course be sure to snip off the point and barb at the bend of the hook for safety reasons.

▶ SOME OF THE MOST ACCURATE CASTERS have impaired vision yet hit the targets consistently. My mentors, Frank Steel, Clare Bryan and George Applegren did not have good vision, yet they were extremely accurate casters (Frank and George shot perfect scores in the Dry Fly Event at a National). How did they do it? They practiced and learned to strip exactly three feet of line from the reel. Let's say that Target D is 11 feet from Target B. While false casting, they would strip four times (12 feet) and then take in one foot. There are times when this stripping method can come in handy in fishing. I fish some Wisconsin trout streams at night, and I prefer no moon at all. Each season I locate several big browns during the day, but these fish feed almost entirely at night. They are difficult to cast to, because they generally

live where there is plenty of brush and overhanging branches. These browns are cagey all right. It's difficult enough to cast to them during the day without hanging up, let alone on a dark night. Here's what I do: During the day I scout the places that harbor the big browns and figure out exactly where to stand to get the right drift and angle. Finding and "marking" this spot is crucial. I use a 9-foot leader and start with about two feet of fly line beyond the rod tip. Then I make a number of casts to determine the exact amount of line I need to reach the "target" without snagging. If I need, say, an additional 24 feet to reach my "target" I strip eight times (three-foot lengths) and PRESTO! I'm usually exactly where I want to be. I then go to the place at night, wait for a hatch and make my cast. I usually have four or five such "stakeouts" that I visit every night. Yes, I've been successful. Of course, I lose some of these big brutes, because of snags, but at least I hook them.

▶ YOU WILL NOTICE an absence of various "supplemental" casts (such as the curve, reach and other casts). I believe it's important to learn the standard cast and strive for accuracy and throwing a narrow, controlled loop. Once that is learned, all the other casts can be easily incorporated. Personally, in almost 60 years of steady fly fishing for trout in many places, I can't recall having to use most of these "exotic casts" very often. The exception is the "Lazy-S" cast, which puts slack in the line to avoid drag, and is easily accomplished by wiggling the rod tip from side to side on the forward (presentation) cast. Once you've mastered the standard cast, learn the others if you like (most how-to casting books offer detailed explanations on them).

▶ AFTER YOU FEEL THAT YOU have developed sufficient proficiency in these events and disciplines, I highly recommend practicing some of the accuracy events while sitting in a chair. Reason? If you ever fish from a canoe or a light craft, safety and common sense dictate that you cast sitting down. I have some great stories on this, but I'll save them for another time.

► THROUGHOUT THESE PAGES, I've mentioned the importance of keeping track of your scores. The reason is, that besides offering a gauge for your progress, you are, in effect, competing against yourself and this competition will fuel your drive to succeed. You can keep track of your scores in a little notebook or devise a more formal scorecard as per the illustration.

Casting Scorecard for _____

| Date | Event | Score | Weather/Comments |
|---|---|---|---|
| 5/05/05 | Dry Fly | 82 | Windy, bright |
| 5/11/05 | Dry Fly | 88 | Calm, overcast |
| 5/13/05 | Dry Fly | 91 | Bright...broke 90! |
| 5/14/05 | Bass Bug | 84 | Missed the long ones |
| 5/20/05 | Angler's Dist. | 122 ft. | Calm... |
| 6/5/05 | Bass Bug | 88 | Windy, overcast |
| 6/14/05 | One-Hand | 143 ft. | Nice wind; humid |
| 7/11/05 | Bass Bug | 80 | Tough casting. windy |
| 7/16/05 | One Minute | 9 targets | Lots of fun |
| 7/18/05 | Level 8 | 60 pts. | Tried new leader |
|  |  |  |  |
|  |  |  |  |

► THE FUTURE OF CASTING? From the late 1800s to about 1950, tackle manufacturers and the angling press promoted tournament casting very aggressively. *Field & Stream, Outdoor Life* and other major publications often published full-length articles on casting. Owners of split-bamboo rod companies (such as Hardy, Leonard, Hawes, etc.), as well as others associated in the tackle business (e.g., Tony Acceta, Fred Arbogast, Bill Jamison, Dave Abercrombie and Ezra Fitch), vigorously competed in fly-casting accuracy and distance tournaments. (Cliff Netherton chronicles these significant events in his two fascinating books, *History of the Sport of Casting: Early Times* and, *History of the Sport of Casting: Golden Times*).

What about the past fishing writers and experts? George M. L. LaBranche, Seth Green, Reuben Wood, Edward R. Hewitt–four of the most influential fly fishermen–were passionately engaged in tournament casting.

During the 1940s and 1950s, just about every major city had a casting club. For example, there were eight casting clubs in Chicago and a half dozen other clubs within short driving distance of Chicago. In Milwaukee, there was even an "industrial league" for casters, in which the huge corporations (e.g., Allis Chambers) sponsored casting teams. Casting historian Cliff Netherton refers to these years as "the golden years of casting."

Can tournament casting ever regain its popularity of decades past? Perhaps not. At least not to the extent it once enjoyed. I'm convinced that there will be a resurgence in casting practice (for the lack of a better phrase) and new casting clubs will be formed. The word "tournament" seems to scare off anglers—despite the fact that many of them are avid golfers and highly competitive in other activities.

I hope that the tackle manufacturing and sportfishing community will embrace and promote tournament casting. For instance, there are the popular Bassmaster CastingKids and other programs that encourage youngsters to cast. But is there a program that takes them to the next step? Not that I know of. The sportfishing industry is ignoring a very important link, if it's interested in converting kids into anglers and thus eventually increasing the sport's popularity and its own profits.

*That's it! Keep casting!*

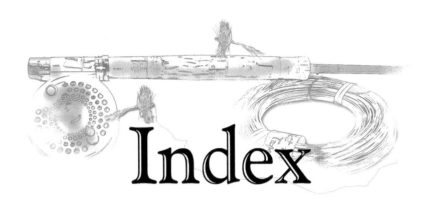

# Index

For additional copies, questions or comments:

Jim Chapralis

***AnglingMatters***

 3518 Davis, Evanston, IL 60203

jchapralis@ameritech.net    847.673.3915

$16.95 + $2.50 (postage and handling) =  $19.45